SANTA
HIKING GUIDE

BY BOB D'ANTONIO

WESTCLIFFE PUBLISHERS

westcliffepublishers.com

International Standard Book Number: 1-56579-500-8

Text and Photography copyright: Bob D'Antonio, 2004. All rights reserved.

Editor: Elizabeth Train
Designer: Carol Pando
Production Manager: Craig Keyzer

Published by:
Westcliffe Publishers, Inc.
P.O. Box 1261
Englewood, CO 80150
westcliffepublishers.com

Printed in the USA by: Vaughn Printing, Inc.

Library of Congress Cataloging-in-Publication Data:
D'Antonio, Bob.
    Santa Fe-Taos hiking guide / text and photography by Bob D'Antonio
      p. cm.
    Includes index.
    ISBN 1-56579-500-8
     1. Hiking—New Mexico—Santa Fe Region—Guidebooks. 2. Hiking—New Mexico—Taos Region—Guidebooks. 3. Santa Fe Region (N.M.)—Guidebooks. 4. Taos Region (N.M.)—Guidebooks. I. Title.

GV199.42.N62S253 2004
917.89'560454—dc22   2004043049

*For more information about other fine books and calendars from Westcliffe Publishers, please contact your local bookstore, call us at 1-800-523-3692, write for our free color catalog, or visit us on the Web at **www.westcliffepublishers.com.***

Please Note: Risk is always a factor in backcountry and high-mountain travel. Many of the activities described in this book can be dangerous, especially when weather is adverse or unpredictable, and when unforeseen events or conditions create a hazardous situation. The author has done his best to provide the reader with accurate information about backcountry travel, as well as to point out some of its potential hazards. It is the responsibility of the users of this guide to learn the necessary skills for safe backcountry travel, and to exercise caution in potentially hazardous areas. The author and publisher disclaim any liability for injury or other damage caused by backcountry traveling or performing any other activity described in this book.

Cover Photo: Backpacker on Hamilton Mesa in Pecos Wilderness Area, Truchas Peaks in the background. Photo by William Stone.
Previous Page: Nambe Lake, the turnaround point of Hike 19.
Opposite: Steep hiking out of the Rio Grande Gorge.

CONTENTS

Taos Area Hikes

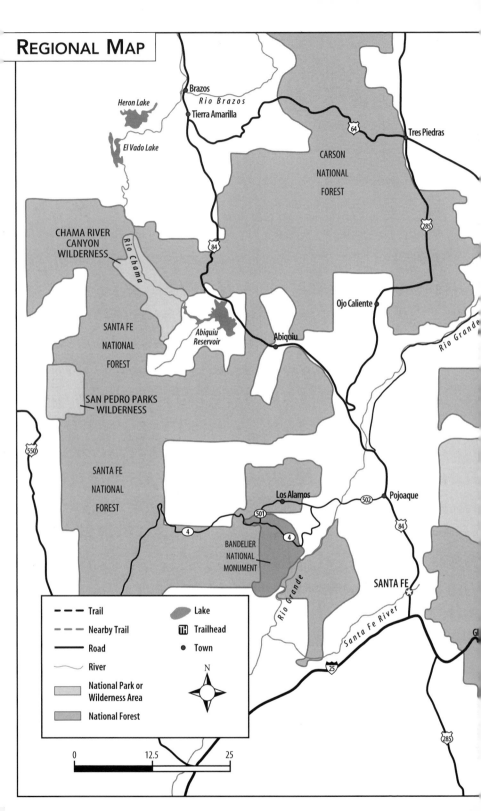

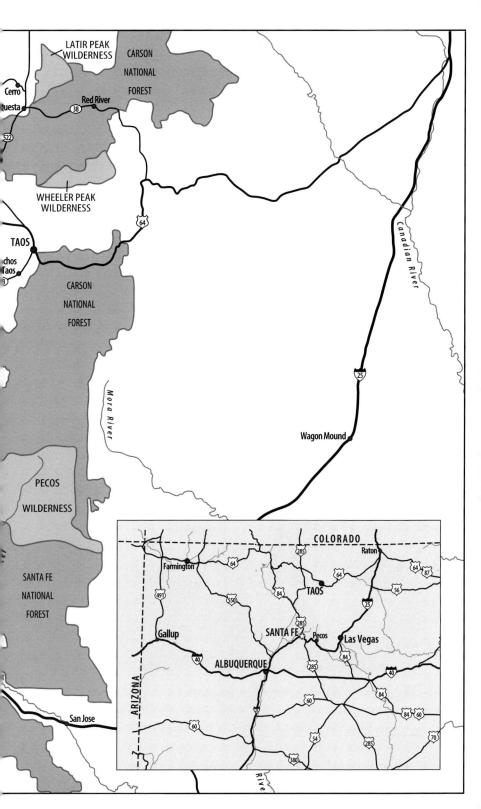

INTRODUCTION

The mountains and high desert surrounding the beautiful cities of Santa Fe and Taos contain a plethora of excellent hiking trails unequaled in the state of New Mexico. From towering alpine peaks to sage-covered mesas—with everything in between—hiking in northern New Mexico will satisfy the appetite of any outdoor enthusiast.

Hikes 1–25 are within an hour's drive of Santa Fe. They range from beautiful high-desert trails through dry arroyos and cacti-covered hills to climbs through evergreen forests, leading to the tops of broad, towering peaks, such as 12,661-foot Santa Fe Baldy. Hikes 26–52, within an hour of Taos, range from a trip into the deep chasm of the Rio Grande Gorge to the top of Wheeler Peak, which, at 13,161 feet above sea level, is the highest point in the state.

Along with beautiful terrain, Taos and Santa Fe themselves offer rich and diverse culture, a unique art scene, historic sites and buildings, and an eclectic collection of people. Welcome to the beauty and diversity that is northern New Mexico, and enjoy your time exploring these wonderful lands.

San Miguel Mission Church, Santa Fe

Opposite: *Paintbrush, Lake Peak, Pecos Wilderness*
Photo by Mike Butterfield

How to Use this Guide

This guide describes 52 easily accessible hikes within 45 miles of either Santa Fe or Taos. The categories below provide detailed information to help you select a hike that fits your ability, time frame, and hiking preference. Overview maps show hike locations relative to each town and to each other. This helps you find a hike in the area you wish to explore and enables you to link several routes for a longer backcountry experience.

Highlights:	These short descriptions give a sense of what might be seen from the trail, such as wildflowers, wildlife, the terrain you will experience, and what makes this hike worth doing.
Distance:	One-way distances are given for out-and-back hikes; round-trip mileage is provided for loop routes. I used a Garmin GPS system to gather information for all of these hikes. Keep in mind, however, that the margin of error on mileage can be as great as 10 percent.
Trail Rating:	Each trail is rated in terms of its difficulty.
Hiking Time:	This is a rough estimate of the time it might take a person in good physical condition to complete each hike. The information should only be used as a guideline, as hikers, trail conditions, and hiking styles differ.
Location:	The approximate distance to the trailhead, from either Santa Fe or Taos, is given for each hike.
Elevation:	The first figure noted is the starting elevation of the hike; the second figure represents the highest point (or in some cases the lowest point) reached on the route.
Season:	This section recommends the best times of the year for doing each hike. However, feel free to do any of the routes in this book at any time of year, weather and fortitude permitting. Bear in mind that most of the hikes above 10,000 feet will be covered in snow from late October to early May.
Maps:	Detailed maps depict each hike in this book. These maps were designed with the help of BLM, DeLorme, Forest Service, Trail Illustrated, and USGS maps as well as various other sources. However, it is always a good idea to bring additional maps to complement those in the book. With this in mind, the best maps to consult for each hike are provided for your reference.
Management:	A landowner or land-management agency is listed for each hike so that you can obtain up-to-date information about trail conditions and closures. Contact information for these agencies is provided in Appendix A.
Directions:	Detailed driving directions, from either Santa Fe or Taos to the various trailheads, are given for each hike.

MILEAGE/KEY POINTS

Each trail is described in terms of mileage and way points—from signs and trail junctions to natural markers such as summits, ridgelines, saddles, lakes, and streams. This breakdown helps you ensure that you are, quite literally, on the right track.

An overall description of the character of each hike, including scenery, natural attractions, and landmarks, gives a sense of the trail and helps define the route. This description reflects the Mileage/Key Points chart for easy cross-reference, but also provides information ranging from the history of the area to quality of the trail surface.

Photo by Mike Butterfield

The Rio en Medio runs through the Santa Fe Ski Basin.

ON THE TRAIL

TRAIL MANNERS

My time in the woods is very important to me. I particularly enjoy the solitude and beauty that hiking in the backcountry brings. I recommend taking your time when exploring the outdoors. Don't always hurry to get *somewhere*. Stop often, and spend time trying to blend with your surroundings. Listen to the wind, the trees, and the animals in these beautiful areas. Sometimes it is best to get *nowhere* and, instead, to feel like you are part of the natural world.

I strive to ensure that my presence in the woods will leave little, if any, negative impact. Our public lands are precious, and we must tread on them lightly, both for the sake of those who follow and for the welfare of the land itself. It is important to keep the principles of Leave No Trace in mind whenever you enter the backcountry, and to treat the land with utmost care.

▢PRINCIPLES OF LEAVE NO TRACE

- Plan Ahead and Prepare
- Travel and Camp on Durable Surfaces
- Dispose of Waste Properly
- Leave What You Find
- Minimize Campfire Impacts
- Respect Wildlife
- Be Considerate of Other Visitors

For more information, visit www.lnt.org.

▢TRAIL USE

Most of the routes described in this book are on multi-use trails. This means that you can expect to see other trail users—from bikers and equestrians to recreational vehicles—on your hike. (However, trails in designated wilderness areas are closed to motorized vehicles and mountain bikes.) Always give horses and pack animals, such as llamas and burros, the right-of-way. Quick movements and loud noise might frighten them, so please approach these creatures with caution. Expect to see hunters on the trail in autumn, and wear brightly colored clothing to make your presence known.

▢HUMAN IMPACT

Your time in the backcountry should have little, if any, negative impact. Stay on the trail, and always follow switchbacks—don't cut across them.

Leave wildflowers alone and in place for the next hiker to see.

If you are a smoker, put out your cigarette butts properly and take them with you. Be careful with fire of all sorts. Wildfires are a real danger in New Mexico, and a lot of them result from human carelessness.

Dispose of human waste properly. Do your duty away from water sources and campsites. Dig a "cat hole" at least 6 inches deep, put your waste in the hole, and cover it well. Always pack out your toilet paper; do not leave it behind for someone else to find!

◻CAMPING

Most of the hikes in this book are day hikes, but some can be done as overnight trips. If you choose to camp, please follow these suggestions in order to avoid impacting the area during your stay.

- Camp at least 300 feet away from lakes, streams, rivers, and all other water sources.
- Pick a site that is established and level.
- Use well-established fire rings or, better yet, forget about the fire. Modern stoves are much more efficient and leave no impact on the ground. Never cut trees to use as firewood.
- Carry out all of your trash and, if necessary, the trash of others. It takes very little effort to keep a campsite clean, and it feels good to leave an area undisturbed, or even better than you found it.

◻DOGS ON THE TRAIL

Dogs can be wonderful hiking companions. I bring my Labrador, Nala, with me all the time. She is a well-behaved dog and has spent a lot of time in the woods. She in not aggressive and is friendly toward other dogs and people. Not all dogs are like Nala, however. If a dog does not listen to commands, it is better left at home, both for its safety and for the safety and enjoyment of others.

Lost Lake, Wheeler Peak Wilderness

◻WILDLIFE

The more time you spend in the woods, the better chance you have of seeing wild creatures in their natural habitats. Enjoy your encounters with wildlife and let them continue to roam the woods on their own terms, not yours.

Black bears inhabit the backcountry near Santa Fe and Taos. I have had three encounters with bears along the trail, and all of them have been amicable. Give bears a wide berth and an easy escape route, and stay particularly far away from a mother with cubs. If you are camping, keep food and other items with strong odors in a sack and hang it from a tree at least 10 to 15 feet off of the ground. If a bear does lay claim to your food, let the bear have its day so you can have another.

Snakes often sun themselves on the trail, especially at lower elevations. Most are harmless, and will slither away before you come near. *Rattlesnakes are not aggressive* and will not strike unless you happen to step upon or provoke them. If you encounter a rattlesnake on the trail, give it space and leave it alone. They are important predators and deserve respect.

There are many ways to treat snakebites and most are quite controversial and far beyond my expertise. Here is my best advice: If you are bitten by a snake, *get help right away.*

Insects are a pain-in-the–you-know-what. Fortunately, they are more of a nuisance than a health threat in the Santa Fe and Taos area. Mosquitoes hatch after heavy summer rains and can be particularly prevalent in mountain areas near lakes and streams. Repellent with a high percentage of DEET should keep the little buggers at bay.

Ticks are not much of an issue in the Santa Fe and Taos areas. In fact, I've never seen a tick when hiking in the woods of northern New Mexico. However, tick bites can cause problems. Some tick species carry serious diseases such as Rocky Mountain spotted fever and Lyme disease. Again, repellent should deter these creatures, but it is also a good idea to check yourself for ticks after you've been hiking.

AUTHOR'S ADVICE

The number one principle of Leave No Trace is **BE PREPARED**. You alone can make your trip into the backcountry memorable—in every sense of the word. Learn how to use a map, and consider bringing a GPS system with you on your trip into the backcountry. Give a detailed copy of your itinerary to a friend or family member before you leave. Make an equipment checklist for your hike, and check it!

Always carry some sort of backpack, whether you are going for a short hike or a longer trek. Check the weather forecast, and choose your provisions with the worst-case scenario in mind. As the saying goes, "expect the best but be prepared for the worst." Bring foul-weather gear and extra clothing. Sun block and a hat are a must for protection from the sun, even when it's cold. Bring water and food to consume while you hike, and include extra portions of both for emergencies. Pick a hike to match your abilities, and carry good maps of your route. Be sure you are physically fit and well acclimated before trying a hike at higher elevations. You are more likely to enjoy your time hiking these wonderful trails if you are prepared for whatever lies ahead.

▪EQUIPMENT

Most of the hikes in this book are day hikes and do not require a great deal of equipment. Nevertheless, some tools and equipment will enhance and make your outing more enjoyable. Always pack matches or a lighter, an emergency blanket or shelter, a pocketknife or mutli-purpose tool, a first aid kit, a whistle, a map, and a compass. I've said it once, and I'll say it again: Carry extra food and water. The greatest assets that you can bring into the backcountry, however, are common sense and a grasp of your limitations.

Kiosk at the start of the Winsor Creek Loop.

▪SHOES

Footwear can contribute to a wonderful, memorable hiking experience or a horrible nightmare. Blisters and sore feet will keep you from enjoying the beautiful scenery and from reaching your destination or exploring new trails. The length of a hike and the condition of the trail can determine what kind of footwear is appropriate. On shorter hikes and on smooth trails, a light hiking shoe will suffice. Longer hikes with rugged, rocky trails require a sturdy hiking shoe or boot with firmer soles for stability and adequate ankle support.

Make sure your footwear is properly broken in, and don't ever attempt a long hike on a rough trail in brand new shoes. Proper socks are also important, particularly for long hikes. A thin liner and wool/synthetic sock combination will wick perspiration from your feet and help reduce the friction that leads to blisters.

▪WEATHER

Most problems in the outdoors arise from sudden or severe weather changes. Northern New Mexico enjoys a staggering 300 days of sunshine a year and, for the most part, has stable weather conditions. That said, the weather here varies from season to season, day to day, and sometimes even from hour to hour. Keep a particularly close eye on the sky when you are hiking in exposed areas at high altitudes.

Summer in Santa Fe and Taos is simply beautiful. The wildflowers are in bloom, and the longer days allow for more time on the trail. Temperatures can reach above 90 degrees during the day and drop to 50 degrees at night. The rainy season begins sometime in mid-July and lasts into September. Storms can be extreme, and lightning is a concern in exposed areas such as high peaks or ridgelines. Though infrequent, snow can fall in the higher elevations during summer months. If you are hiking in the high country, be prepared for sudden weather changes and varied temperatures.

Fall is mostly a time of stable weather and mild temperatures. This is a beautiful time to be in the high mountains, as the golden aspen light up the hillsides. Fall can also bring unstable weather and heavy, wet snow. What starts out as a calm, mellow autumn day in the mountains can quickly change into your worst nightmare. Bring extra clothing and be aware of weather patterns.

Winter brings shorter days and colder temperatures, especially in the high county. Hikers venturing into the winter backcountry **must** be prepared for severe conditions and slow traveling times due to weather and snowy conditions. However, don't let the harsh conditions deter you from spending time on the trail during the winter months. Adventurous, well-prepared hikers will enjoy great solitude and beauty during the winter.

Spring has the temperament of a moody toddler. One minute it's fine, the next it's completely out of control. Be prepared for sudden weather changes and varied temperatures. High winds can be a problem during the early spring months. Bring extra clothing, and be prepared to shorten your hike due to changes in the weather. Bear in mind that most of the trails in the high country (above 10,000 feet) are still covered with snow in springtime, providing great opportunities to enjoy the trails at lower elevations.

WATER

Proper hydration contributes to an enjoyable and safe hiking experience. It is always important to pack what you think you'll drink, and then some more.

Along with those 300 days of sunshine comes low humidity and a dry, arid climate. Hikers lose water through temperature regulation, heavy breathing, and increased metabolic rates. Make yourself drink water before starting a hike and periodically along the trail. If you become thirsty, that means you are already low on fluids.

Dehydration can lead to heat exhaustion and a more dangerous condition, heat stroke. Warning signs and symptoms include dizziness, rapid pulse, reduced perspiration, general weakness, and sluggishness. A hiker with these symptoms should get out of the sun immediately, find a cool place, drink large quantities of water, and, if possible, pour cold water over his or her head.

That said, the Santa Fe and Taos areas enjoy more substantial amounts of moisture than much of the state, and many of the hikes in this book follow streams or are close to lakes. I always bring a filtration system with me on the trail. These nifty little devices are quite light and easy to use. Just remember that this system only works if there is water to be filtered. For this reason, I've mentioned springs and other water sources in the text, and rivers, streams, creeks, and lakes are depicted on the maps. Try to get your water from springs or a good distance (and preferably upstream) from trails and camping sites.

◻YOUR PHYSICAL CONDITION

A lot of the trails in this book feature significant elevation gains and steep terrain. Do not attempt a hike that is way beyond your physical condition and ability. You are only going to regret it, and it may dampen your enthusiasm for future hikes. Choose a route that is right for you to ensure that your hike will be a fun and enjoyable adventure.

If you are new to hiking, begin with one of the easy hikes in this book and work your way up from there. Pace yourself and stay within your abilities. Remember that a mile of hiking on a flat, smooth trail is much easier and takes a lot less time than a mile on a rugged, rocky trail at a high elevation. Also know when to call it quits. If you are suffering on a hike, turn around and head back to the trailhead and your car. The trail will always be there, and the purpose of hiking in the mountains is to enjoy yourself!

◻ALTITUDE SICKNESS

Altitude sickness usually occurs above 7,000 feet above sea level. (Most of the hikes in this book start at 7,000 feet and climb to higher elevations.) Symptoms are dizziness, lack of energy, nausea, headaches, and shortness of breath. If you begin to feel any of these symptoms, stop hiking, rest, eat some food, drink some fluids, and drop back down to a lower elevation.

One of the sure-fire ways to avoid altitude sickness is to properly acclimate before attempting a hike at altitude. If you are coming from lower elevations, spend a few days in Santa Fe or Taos casually walking around before hitting the trail.

◻HIKING WITH CHILDREN

Several hikes in this book are especially suited for young children and make for an enjoyable family experience. Some of the best times my wife and I have spent in the backcountry have been with our children. With that said, we have also had some very trying times hiking and backpacking with the youngsters.

Pick a hike that is suitable for your child or children's ability and attention span. Young children become tired easily and lose interest if there is little to do or see. Bring extra food, water, clothing, and *lots* of patience. Also remember that children move at a slower pace and look at the outside world differently than adults. A butterfly, log, tree, rock, or bird might be of great interest to a child, and lakes and streams provide endless opportunities for entertainment and discovery. Let little ones explore and move along at their own pace, but keep a watchful eye. Most children will enjoy their time in the woods if they are not pushed beyond the limits of their physical ability or attention span.

☐LOSING YOUR WAY

Most of the hikes in this book are well marked and easy to follow. However, things can go wrong, and one can lose the path of a trail very easily. Pay attention to landmarks, and be aware of your surroundings. If you lose your way, stop and regroup. Try to retrace your steps back to a familiar trail junction or landmark. If all else fails, stay put and wait for help to come to you. Always leave your itinerary with family or friends before you set off for the trail.

Awesome hiking and great views on the Big Arsenic Spring Trail.

LIFE ZONES IN NORTHERN NEW MEXICO

Northern New Mexico has diverse weather, ecosystems, and topography. Five of the seven life zones are within a 90-minute drive of either Santa Fe or Taos, and over 2.5 million acres of federal land, including three designated wilderness areas, are open to the public in this region. For the hiking enthusiast, this means a wide selection of wonderful trails can be easily and conveniently enjoyed throughout the year.

The country around Santa Fe and Taos is where the high desert and Rocky Mountains meet. The rounded foothills around each town are covered in piñon and juniper trees and support a mixture of desert plants such as yucca, agave, sagebrush, chamiso, cholla, and prickly pear cacti. This area is a classic example of the **Upper Sonoran Zone**.

As you travel higher into the hills, tall ponderosa pines and low-growing mountain mahogany define the **Transition Zone**. The name implies a change from the arid desert to the lush forest. Though more moisture falls in this zone, it still can be quite dry. As you hike through the Transition Zone, you will travel through stands of stately ponderosa pine mixed with quaking aspen and meadows filled with tall, green grasses and colorful wildflowers.

As you ascend into the mountains, you will reach the **Canadian Zone**. Named for its resemblance to the conifer forests of Canada, this life zone consists of Douglas fir, Engelmann spruce, lodgepole pine, subapline fir, and quaking aspen. The trails through this zone are often shaded, cool, and covered in conifer needles.

As you continue to rise in elevation, you will enter the **Hudsonian Zone**, also known as the **Subapline Zone**. This is where the forest meets the tundra, also known as timberline. Engelmann spruce and subapline fir are the most common trees here, but they scarcely resemble their counterparts from lower elevations due to their stunted growth and the flag-like appearance they are given by the harsh elements and severe weather.

Last is the **Arctic-Alpine Zone**. This zone is above timberline and consists of tough, tundra grasses, sedges, and hardy perennial wildflowers. Weather is similar to that of the Hudsonian Zone, but maximum exposure to the harsh elements keeps woody species from surviving. This is one of my favorite life zones due to the open views and wonderful grasses and wildflowers that grow here during the short, summer months.

Opposite: Looking south from Italianos Canyon.
Photo by William Stone

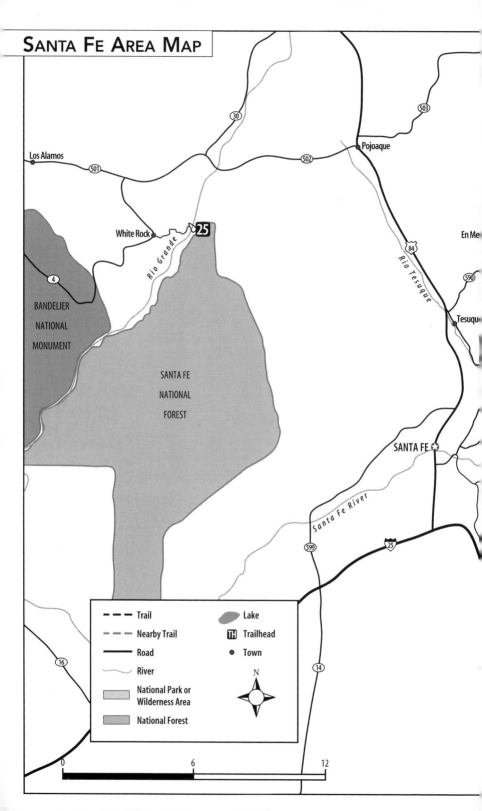

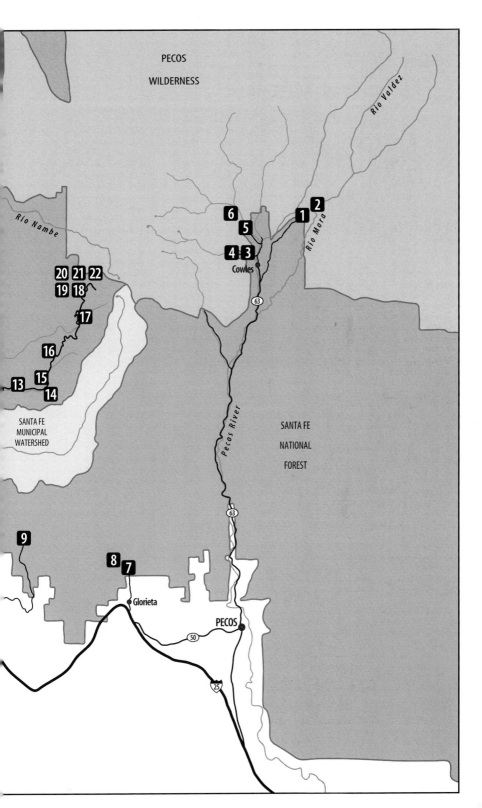

HIKE 1

HAMILTON MESA

HIGHLIGHTS:	The large, open meadow on Hamilton Mesa holds some of the best wildflowers in all of northern New Mexico. The views are also spectacular, making the mesa a wonderful destination for a day hike or overnight trip.
DISTANCE:	5 miles one way
TRAIL RATING:	Moderate
HIKING TIME:	5 to 8 hours
LOCATION:	40 miles northeast of Santa Fe
ELEVATION:	9,400 to 10,600 feet
SEASON:	Early June to late October
MAPS:	Drake Mountain Maps: Mountains of Santa Fe
MANAGEMENT:	Santa Fe National Forest/Pecos Wilderness
DIRECTIONS:	From Santa Fe, head north on I-25 to Exit 299. Cross over the highway, turn right on NM 50, and travel 6 miles to the town of Pecos and the junction with NM 63. Turn left on NM 63 and proceed 18.6 miles to the turnoff for Iron Gate Campground (Forest Road 223). Turn right and continue over a rough 4.4 miles to the campground and trailhead. There is a $2.00 fee for day use. Avoid FR 223 during and after heavy precipitation.

This is one of the best hikes in the Pecos Wilderness for wildflower viewing and open views to the towering summits of Lake Peak, Santa Fe Baldy, Pecos Baldy, the Truchas Peaks, and Jicarita Peak. The trail begins at the northeast corner of the campground, near the bathrooms and the Forest Service kiosk. Consult this kiosk for up-to-date information, and be sure to sign in before hitting the trail.

MILEAGE/KEY POINTS
0.0 Trailhead and kiosk.
0.4 Go left at a trail junction.
1.0 Continue straight on Trail 249.
1.7 Reach a gate.
2.1 Hike's high point.
3.5 Reach a junction with Trail 260; go left.
4.5 Reach a gate and junction with Trail 270. Go left, continuing on Trail 260.
5.0 Cross a bridge over the Pecos River.

Trail 249 climbs gently through a forest of mixed conifers and lovely aspen trees. Reach a trail junction at 0.4 mile, and go left along a ridgeline with great views down to the Rio Mora and Mora Flats. Drop down for a short distance and then climb up to another trail junction. (Trail 250 goes right and down to Mora Flats—a popular route that sees heavy foot and horse traffic.) Continue straight on Trail 249, up through Gambel oak and aspen trees, to a gate at the 1.7-mile mark. Travel past the gate and climb gently to Hamilton Mesa.

You might want to get out the camera when the Pecos Peaks appear to the west. This section of the trail really deserves to be traveled at a slow pace. The beautiful vistas and vibrant wildflowers will keep your eyes moving faster than your legs. Hamilton Mesa is host to more than 30 species of brightly colored wildflowers during the summer. Wild iris, paintbrush, gentian, spiderwort, and cinquefoil are just a few of the plants that thrive here.

The trail climbs up to a high point and then becomes level as it cuts through the tall meadow grasses. Pleasant hiking and spectacular views prevail for the next 1.5 miles. Patches of conifer and aspen add to the overall beauty of this alpine meadow.

Arrive at a signed trail junction in the open meadow at the 3.5-mile mark. It's time to make a decision, as this is a good turnaround point for those who want a shorter hike. Trail 249 continues straight and reaches Pecos Falls in 4 miles. To reach Beatty's Cabin, however, go left on Beatty's Trail 260 and drop down into a mixed-conifer forest on a winding path to the junction with Trail 270 and a gate. Continue on Trail 260, to the left, for another half-mile, and cross a log bridge over the Pecos River. You'll soon enter the meadow where George Beatty's cabin once stood. This is a wonderful spot to enjoy some lunch before retracing the route back to the trailhead or to camp if you're planning to stay for more than a day.

1 HAMILTON MESA

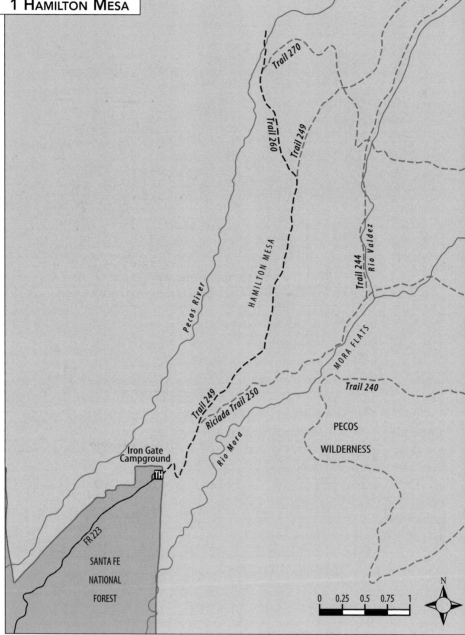

Trail 270

Trail 260

Trail 249

Pecos River

HAMILTON MESA

Trail 244

Rio Valdez

MORA FLATS

Trail 240

Trail 249

Riciada Trail 250

Rio Mora

PECOS

WILDERNESS

Iron Gate
Campground

TH

FR 223

SANTA FE

NATIONAL

FOREST

N

0   0.25   0.5   0.75   1

HIKE 2

MORA FLATS

HIGHLIGHTS:	Beautiful campsites, wildflowers, good fly-fishing, and the crystal clear Rio Valdez highlight this short excursion into the Pecos Wilderness.
DISTANCE:	3.8 miles one way
TRAIL RATING:	Moderate
HIKING TIME:	5 to 8 hours
LOCATION:	40 miles northeast of Santa Fe
ELEVATION:	9,200 to 9,600 feet
SEASON:	Early June to late October
MAPS:	Drake Mountain Maps: Mountains of Santa Fe
MANAGEMENT:	Santa Fe National Forest/Pecos Wilderness
DIRECTIONS:	From Santa Fe, head north on I-25 to Exit 299. Cross over the highway, turn right on NM 50, and travel 6 miles to the town of Pecos and the junction with NM 63. Turn left on NM 63 and travel 18.6 miles to the turnoff for Iron Gate Campground (Forest Road 223). Turn right and travel a rough 4.4 miles to the campground and trailhead. There is a $2.00 fee for day use. Avoid FR 223 during and after heavy precipitation.

One of the best wildflower hikes in the Pecos Wilderness, this route makes an easy overnight trip for the novice backpacker. This hike shares the same beginning as the hike to Hamilton Mesa, beginning at the northeast corner of the campground, near the bathrooms and the Forest Service kiosk. Consult this kiosk for up-to-date information, and be sure to sign in before hitting the trail.

MILEAGE/KEY POINTS

0.0 Trailhead and kiosk.
0.4 Go left at a trail junction.
1.0 Go right on Trail 250 (Riciada Trail).
2.3 Reach a gate.
3.3 Arrive at Mora Flats and a trail junction with Trail 240; continue straight.
3.8 Arrive at a trail junction in a beautiful open meadow, the turnaround point.

Trail 249 climbs gently through aspen and conifer trees. When you reach a trail junction at 0.4 mile, go left along a ridgeline with great views down to the Rio Mora and Mora Flats. Drop down for a short distance and then climb up to another trail junction. Follow Trail 250 to the right and down to Mora Flats, crossing an exposed hill. Wildflowers grow profusely on the hillsides and along the trail. Paintbrush, wild iris, lupine, wild geranium, and wild strawberry are just a few of the flowers that you'll find blooming here during the summer months.

At the 2.3-mile mark, you'll pass through a gate—make sure you close it—and begin a steep descent on switchbacks down to Mora Flats. In no time, you'll reach a junction. (Trail 240 shoots off to the right, where excellent campsites can be found.) Continue straight, enjoying open views, beautiful wildflowers, and tall grass. Hiking is flat and pleasant as the meadow becomes wider. You'll reach a trail junction at the 3.8-mile mark—the turnaround point for this hike. Mora Flats is a wonderful place to explore and enjoy for a few days, with great fishing and trails surrounding the flats.

If you'd like to continue hiking from this point, go straight at the trail junction (now you'll be on Trail 244) to reach the Rio Valdez, where the path hugs the stream and climbs up to a junction with Trail 270. This adds about 2 more miles to the hike and provides more opportunities for fly-fishing along the beautiful stream.

2 MORA FLATS

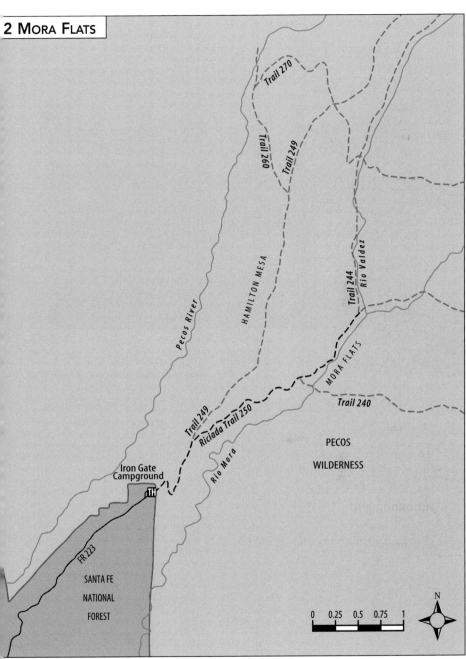

Stewart Lake

Highlights:	Open views, wildflowers, mountain tarns, and great fly-fishing accent this popular route, which creeps along a beautiful ridgeline high above the Winsor Creek drainage to lovely Stewart Lake.
Distance:	5.4 miles one way
Trail Rating:	Moderate to strenuous
Hiking Time:	4 to 7 hours
Location:	40 miles northeast of Santa Fe
Elevation:	9,900 to 11,120 feet
Season:	Early June to late October
Maps:	Drake Mountain Maps: Mountains of Santa Fe; USGS: Cowles
Management:	Santa Fe National Forest/Pecos Wilderness
Directions:	From Santa Fe, head north on I-25 to Exit 299. Cross over the highway, turn right onto NM 50, and travel 6 miles to the town of Pecos and a junction with NM 63. Turn left, and proceed 20.2 miles to Cowles. Make a left turn over the Pecos River and a quick left into the Cowles Ponds parking area.

The trail to Stewart Lake makes for a long day hike or a more relaxing overnight trip. I recommend doing the route as a multi-day excursion in order to enjoy the lake and the surrounding sights. This is one of the nicest and well-maintained trails in the Pecos Wilderness.

From the parking area, cross the road and reach the trailhead and a Forest Service

MILEAGE/KEY POINTS

0.0 Trailhead and bathrooms. Go right on Trail 31.
0.5 Small meadow.
1.0 Reach the Pecos Wilderness boundary.
2.5 Open views.
4.0 Small stream crossing.
5.0 Junction with the Skyline Trail 251.
5.2 Reach a small tarn and wooden bridge.
5.4 Arrive at Stewart Lake.

kiosk. Be sure to sign in, then follow the obvious trail heading west. Several trails originate from the kiosk, so pay attention to trail markers. The trail climbs, crossing over FR 103, and reaches a junction with a trail shooting right to the Panchuela Day-Use Area. Continue straight on Trail 271, climbing high above Winsor Creek.

At approximately the 0.5-mile mark, the trail cuts through a small, open meadow with young aspen and summer wildflowers. The trail climbs quickly and reaches the wilderness boundary at the 1.0-mile mark. Beautiful hiking and a gentle grade makes this section of the trail particularly enjoyable. You'll soon reach another meadow filled with beautiful ferns and lovely aspen trees. I once saw a flock of wild turkeys along this section of the trail, so keep your eyes open for wildlife. I also met Gilbert, a local man who was out bowhunting for elk. Neither Gilbert nor I saw any elk that day (bad for Gilbert, lucky for the elk), but they do frequent the area. The trail continues to climb along the ridge and soon breaks out into the open with great views east to Hamilton Mesa, west to Santa Fe Baldy, Lake Peak, and Penitente Peak, and down into the Winsor Creek drainage. This is a great spot for a short break.

The trail climbs up to a saddle and more views. Beyond the saddle, the trail veers north through a mixed-conifer forest, crosses over a small drainage at the 4.0-mile mark, and then drops down to a junction with the Skyline Trail 251 at mile 5.0. Go left on the Skyline Trail, and you'll quickly reach a small tarn at a wooden bridge. Cross the bridge and climb up to a fork in the trail at a rock cairn. Go right, following the well-worn path up through the dense forest to another bridge and Stewart Lake. The lake is nestled below Santa Fe Baldy and surrounded by dense conifers. Camping is not permitted near the lake, but there are several good sites near the Skyline Trail.

The wildflowers are spectacular beside the lake and in the surrounding basin, making this a very popular route during the summer months. For a little more solitude, try hiking the trail mid-week or after Labor Day, when the summer crowds disappear. Fall is also a great time to enjoy the changing aspen trees and cooler temperatures here.

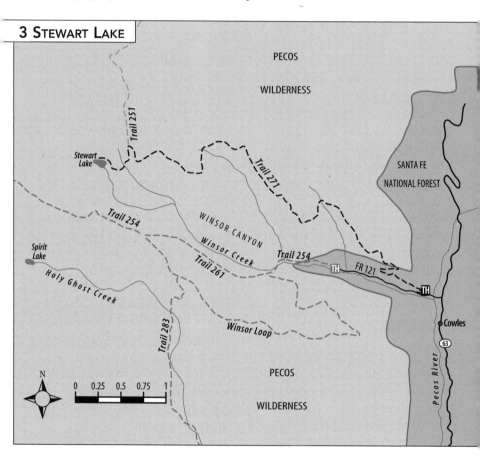

3 STEWART LAKE

HIKE 4

WINSOR CREEK LOOP

HIGHLIGHTS:	This lovely loop follows Trail 261 up along the Winsor Creek drainage and returns on Trail 254, with marvelous wildflowers during the summer months.
DISTANCE:	8.8-mile loop
TRAIL RATING:	Moderate
HIKING TIME:	3 to 6 hours
LOCATION:	40 miles northeast of Santa Fe
ELEVATION:	8,500 to 10,100 feet
SEASON:	Early June to late October
MAPS:	Drake Mountain Maps: Mountains of Santa Fe; USGS: Cowles
MANAGEMENT:	Santa Fe National Forest/Pecos Wilderness
DIRECTIONS:	Head north from Santa Fe on I-25 to Exit 299. Cross over the highway, turn right on NM 50, and travel 6 miles to the town of Pecos and a junction with NM 63. Turn left and travel 20.2 miles to Cowles. Make a left turn over the Pecos River and travel 1.3 miles to the trailhead and parking.

This is a nice loop that follows the Winsor Creek drainage, quickly gaining elevation on Trail 261 for the first part of the hike then descending on Trail 245 back to Winsor Creek and the trailhead. Trail 261 is no longer maintained by the Forest Service, and they encourage hikers and horse traffic to use the maintained Trail 245 (Winsor Trail). However, I like Trail 261 for its shade (the trail is on the north side of the canyon) and quick access to other trails and lakes near by.

MILEAGE/KEY POINTS
0.0 Trailhead, kiosk, and bathrooms. Follow Trail 254 along Winsor Creek.
1.0 Cross Winsor Creek.
1.1 Go right, following Trail 261 beside the creek.
2.8 Reach a junction with Trail 254; go left.
4.3 Reach a junction with Trail 283; bear left.
7.8 Back at Winsor Creek.
8.8 Back at the trailhead.

Sign in at the kiosk near the parking lot, then begin the hike by following Trail 254 into the mouth of Winsor Canyon. Lovely Winsor Creek will be on your left. The trail quickly enters a beautiful meadow, and tall willows line the creek while summer wildflowers grow in the midst of bright green grass.

At the 1.0-mile mark, the trail crosses Winsor Creek and meets Trail 261. Trail 254 goes up and to the left, but you'll continue straight along the creek and through the willows on Trail 261. At the 1.3-mile mark, the trail veers left away from the creek and starts to climb in earnest. Once you've crossed the logs over a small drainage, the route becomes quite rocky. After navigating around several downed trees, you'll soon arrive at a junction with Trail 254. (Stewart Lake lies a mere mile to the north and can be easily accessed by Skyline Trail 251.)

Turn onto Trail 254 and begin descending along a ridgeline on a smooth path to a large meadow and the junction with Holy Ghost Trail 283, which goes right and drops into Holy Ghost Canyon following, not surprisingly, Holy Ghost Creek. Holy Ghost Trail turns right, but you'll bear left on a faint trail, staying on the left side of the meadow, and enter a stand of conifer and aspen.

The trail reaches another meadow, and views open to Cowles and the Pecos River Valley. You will reenter the forest, descend for a mile to a sharp left turn at a switchback, and quickly drop back into Winsor Canyon before arriving at a familiar trail junction. Go right to retrace the route back to the trailhead.

4 WINSOR CREEK LOOP

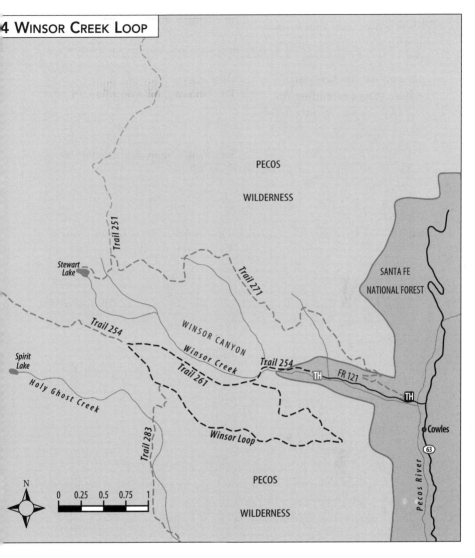

PECOS

WILDERNESS

Trail 251

Stewart
Lake

Trail 271

SANTA FE

NATIONAL FOREST

Trail 254

WINSOR CANYON

Spirit
Lake

Winsor Creek

Trail 254

TH

FR 121

Holy Ghost Creek

Trail 261

TH

Cowles

N

Trail 283

Winsor Loop

63

0   0.25   0.5   0.75   1

PECOS

Pecos River

WILDERNESS

HIKE 5

DOCKWILLER TRAIL

What the Dockwiller Trail lacks in views of the mountains it makes up for in beautiful summer wildflowers, grassy meadows, and towering trees. This is a wonderful hike for those who are not in a particular hurry to get anywhere.

Start by heading northeast and crossing a bridge over Panchuela Creek. Follow the well-worn path along the creek through a forest of stately Douglas firs. Wild iris, geranium, bluebell, and the fragile shooting star are just a few of the colorful beauties that line the trail and grow profusely along the creek in the early summer months.

You'll reach a signed junction at the 0.8-mile mark. The Cave Creek Trail goes straight along the creek, but you will turn right here on the Dockwiller Trail and begin a steep climb up some switchbacks. The trail gains elevation quickly as it reaches the southern end of Mystery Ridge. Enjoy some level hiking through a lovely meadow before reaching another set of steep switchbacks. These will take you to the right and along the Jack's Creek drainage.

MILEAGE/KEY POINTS

0.0 Trailhead and kiosk.

0.8 Reach a junction with Dockwiller Trail 259; go right.

2.0 Reach the first meadow.

3.0 Reach a large, open meadow on the left.

4.0 Reach another large meadow with a small stream at the turnaround point.

HIGHLIGHTS:	Lovely meadows, summer wildflowers, and tall aspen trees that turn a spectacular gold in autumn will reward you on this beautiful hike in the Pecos Wilderness.
DISTANCE:	3 to 5.5 miles one way
TRAIL RATING:	Easy to strenuous (if you do the full 5.5 miles out and back)
HIKING TIME:	2 to 6 hours
LOCATION:	About 42 miles northeast of Santa Fe
ELEVATION:	8,400 to 9,500 feet
SEASON:	Early June to late October
MAPS:	Santa Fe National Forest; USGS: Pecos Wilderness, Cowles
MANAGEMENT:	Santa Fe National Forest/Pecos Wilderness
DIRECTIONS:	From Santa Fe, head north on I-25 to Exit 299. Cross over the highway, turn right on NM 50, and travel 6 miles to the town of Pecos and a junction with NM 63. Turn left and travel 20.2 miles to Cowles. Make another left, crossing the Pecos River, and then a quick right, following the signs to Panchuela Trailhead, at the end of the road. The hike starts here. There is a $2.00 day-use fee.

You'll reach another ridge and enter a larger aspen-filled meadow at the 3.0-mile mark. The trail continues through an aspen forest with little elevation gain. Look around at some of the trees for etching left by travelers from bygone days. The trail soon reaches a large meadow with a small stream running through it—another beautiful spot and the turnaround point for this hike. Spend some time enjoying this lovely place before retracing the route back to the trailhead and your car.

5 DOCKWILLER TRAIL

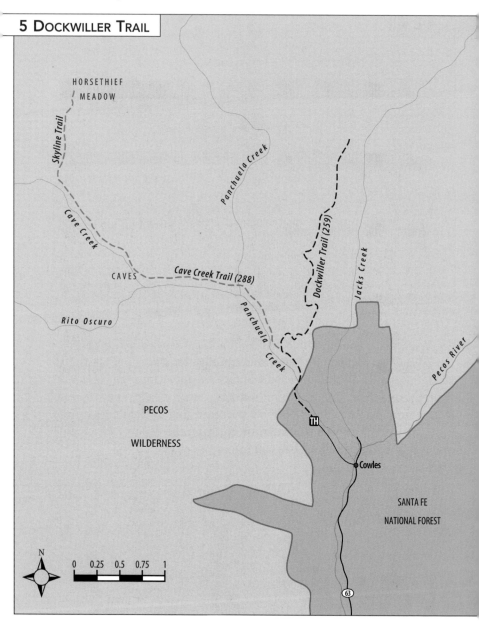

HORSETHIEF
MEADOW

Skyline Trail

Cave Creek

Panchuela Creek

Dockwiller Trail (259)

Jacks Creek

CAVES   Cave Creek Trail (288)

Rito Oscuro

Panchuela Creek

Pecos River

PECOS

WILDERNESS

TH

Cowles

SANTA FE

NATIONAL FOREST

N

0   0.25   0.5   0.75   1

63

HIKE 6

CAVE CREEK TRAIL

HIGHLIGHTS:	Great trout fishing, lush summer vegetation, large, limestone caves, and a "disappearing creek" make this popular hike in the Pecos Wilderness a unique adventure.
DISTANCE:	3.6 miles one way (with option to continue)
TRAIL RATING:	Easy to strenuous (if you do the full 6 miles and back)
HIKING TIME:	1 to 5 hours
LOCATION:	About 42 miles northeast of Santa Fe
ELEVATION:	8,400 to 9,800 feet
SEASON:	Early June to late October
MAPS:	Santa Fe National Forest; USGS: Pecos Wilderness, Cowles
MANAGEMENT:	Santa Fe National Forest/Pecos Wilderness
DIRECTIONS:	From Santa Fe, head north on I-25 to Exit 299. Cross over the highway, turn right on NM 50, and travel 6 miles to the town of Pecos and a junction with NM 63. Turn left and travel 20.2 miles to Cowles. Make another left turn, cross over the Pecos River, and then make a quick right, following signs to Panchuela Trailhead, at the end of the road. The hike starts here. There is a $2.00 day-use fee.

Novice hikers and experts alike will enjoy the trail to the caves along beautiful Panchuela Creek. Beyond the caves, however, the route becomes quite strenuous as the trail climbs up steep switchbacks to a ridgeline before dropping into beautiful

MILEAGE/KEY POINTS
0.0 Trailhead and kiosk.
0.8 Reach a junction with Dockwiller Trail. Continue straight on the Cave Creek Trail 288.
1.5 Cross Panchuela Creek.
1.8 Arrive at the caves.

Horsethief Park at the end of the hike. The park is a wonderful destination for an overnight trip in the summer months.

Start hiking from the west end of the old campground, heading upstream along Panchuela Creek. Cross a bridge and begin a gentle climb along the creek on a well-traveled trail. Pass through a gate and arrive at a junction with the Dockwiller Trail. Continue straight on the Cave Creek Trail through conifer and aspen trees. The vegetation along the creek is quite lush with thick willows and other water-loving plants. Wildflowers flourish here during the summer months and light up the banks of the free-flowing stream.

The trail reaches the confluence of Panchuela Creek and Cave Creek at the 1.5-mile mark. You'll cross the creek and begin hiking along smaller Cave Creek. After about 10 minutes of hiking, you might notice a strange quiet. The sound of the rushing creek, apparent for most of the hike, is all but gone. So is the creek! Continue walking upstream, and look left for the first set of caves. Cave Creek reappears and is funneled into the caves, where it drops underground through limestone walls and surfaces again farther downstream. Two larger caves upstream can be explored with caution. Bring a good light source if you plan to enter the caves, and be careful of the slippery rocks.

Those who simply wish to explore the caves should turn around here. Hikers who want to lengthen their trip can continue heading straight, climbing steeply above Cave Creek on tight, steep switchbacks. Lush vegetation lines the trail with cow parsnip, wild geranium, and lousewort, which grows profusely on the sunny hillside. You'll reach an aspen-filled meadow with lavish ferns and a junction with the Rito Oscuro. This beautiful little spot is a great place to stop before tackling the steep trail ahead.

Strenuous hiking on a fairly steep trail will bring you to a junction with the Skyline Trail 251. Bear right, following the Skyline Trail as it switchbacks along a small drainage and passes through a wildflower-filled meadow up to a ridgeline at the 4.9-mile mark. From here you'll drop steeply into Horsethief Meadow and the end of the hike. Horsethief Meadow is an excellent base camp for climbing Pecos Baldy or for exploring the surrounding lakes and peaks. After enjoying your time in the meadow, retrace the route back to the trailhead and your car.

6 CAVE CREEK TRAIL

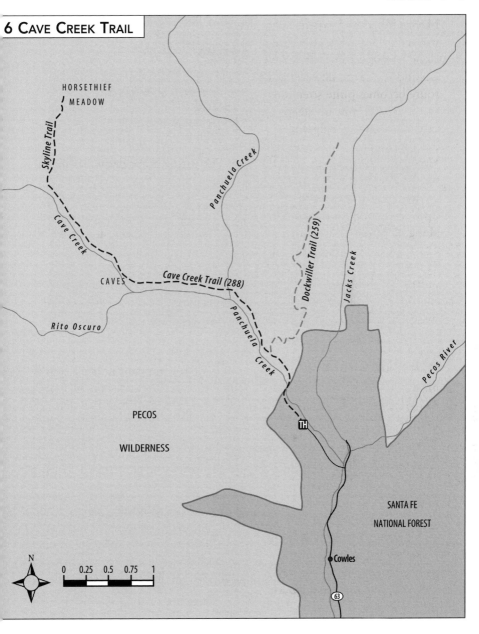

HORSETHIEF
MEADOW

Skyline Trail

Panchuela Creek

Dockwiller Trail (259)

Jacks Creek

Cave Creek

CAVES

Cave Creek Trail (288)

Rito Oscuro

Panchuela Creek

Pecos River

TH

PECOS

WILDERNESS

SANTA FE

NATIONAL FOREST

Cowles

63

N

0   0.25   0.5   0.75   1

HIKE 7

GLORIETA GHOST TOWN

After you've gone through the gate and signed the register, begin walking up the wide road, passing the Glorieta Baldy Trail on the left. Continue straight to another gate at the 0.7-mile mark and a large, open field on the other side. Pass through this gate; you'll see the old Glorieta Baldy Trail on the left.

Begin a gentle climb up the road, which parallels a stream. You will cross this stream several times before you reach the ghost town. During spring runoff, the stream covers sections of the road, which has caused some erosion.

Pleasant hiking will soon bring you to the first of the ruins, on your left. The trail narrows and cuts through an open meadow. The path widens again and brings you to your destination: The Ghost Hotel. All the buildings are now collapsed and you should not disturb or climb on them.

MILEAGE/KEY POINTS

- **0.0** Gate and trailhead.
- **0.1** Pass the Glorieta Baldy Trail on the left.
- **0.3** The road forks; veer left.
- **0.7** Pass through a second gate. Close it!
- **0.8** Pass the old trail to Glorieta Baldy on your left; continue on the road.
- **1.5** The first of several stream crossings.
- **2.9** The first of the old ruins.
- **3.2** The Ghost Hotel and turnaround point.

HIGHLIGHTS:	This old road up to the abandoned ghost town of Glorieta makes a great early-season hike.
DISTANCE:	3.2 miles one way
TRAIL RATING:	Easy to moderate
HIKING TIME:	2 to 3.5 hours
LOCATION:	15 miles northeast of Santa Fe
ELEVATION:	7,500 to 8,450 feet
SEASON:	Early April to late November
MAPS:	Drake Mountain Maps: Mountains of Santa Fe; USGS: Glorieta, McClure Reservoir
MANAGEMENT:	Santa Fe National Forest; private land
DIRECTIONS:	Travel north from Santa Fe on I-25 to Exit 299. Go left over the Interstate and make another left, following the signs for Glorieta Baptist Center. Check in at the entrance, then take your first right and travel 1.4-miles to the trailhead and parking at the ski and bike shop. To access the trailhead, walk down the road and turn left, passing through the RV Park. (The mileage starts at the gate and trailhead.)

You can hike over to and above the towering granite cliffs on the right for better views of the surrounding hills. After you have enjoyed the meadow and views, retrace your route back to the trailhead and your car.

7 GLORIETA GHOST TOWN

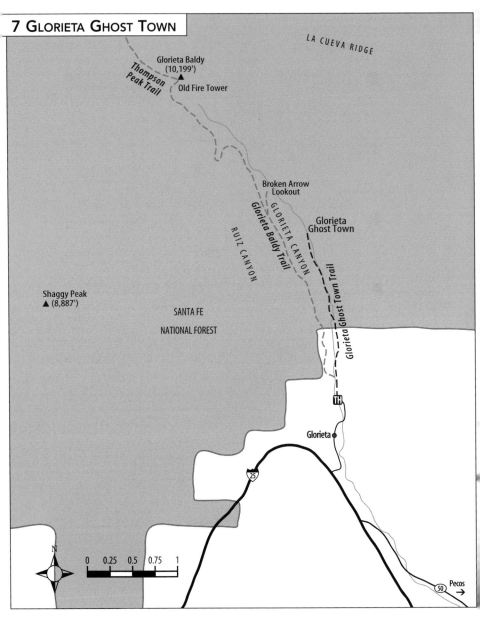

LA CUEVA RIDGE

Glorieta Baldy
(10,199')
Old Fire Tower

Thompson Peak Trail

Broken Arrow
Lookout

Glorieta
Ghost Town

GLORIETA CANYON

Glorieta Baldy Trail

RUIZ CANYON

Shaggy Peak
▲ (8,887')

SANTA FE

NATIONAL FOREST

Glorieta Ghost Town Trail

TH

Glorieta

25

N

0   0.25   0.5   0.75   1

50

Pecos
→

HIKE 8

GLORIETA BALDY TRAIL

HIGHLIGHTS:	Be prepared for a big elevation gain and a strenuous climb on this forested trail to the summit of Glorieta Baldy.
DISTANCE:	5.4 miles one way
TRAIL RATING:	Strenuous
HIKING TIME:	4 to 7 hours
LOCATION:	15 miles northeast of Santa Fe
ELEVATION:	7,500 to 10,199 feet
SEASON:	Early May to mid-November
MAPS:	Drake Mountain Maps: Mountains of Santa Fe; USGS: Glorieta, McClure Reservoir
MANAGEMENT:	Santa Fe National Forest; private land
DIRECTIONS:	Travel north from Santa Fe on I-25 to Exit 299. Go left over the Interstate and make another left following the signs for Glorieta Baptist Center. Check in at the entrance, then take your first right and travel 1.4 miles to the trailhead and parking at the ski and bike shop. To access the trailhead, walk down the road and turn left, passing through the RV Park. (The mileage starts at the gate and trailhead.)

Pass through the gate and travel a few hundred yards up the road to a sign marking the Glorieta Baldy Trail on the left. Go left onto this trail, passing through an area with tall cottonwood trees. The trail climbs up among some large boulders and reaches a gate at the 0.4-mile mark. Look for arrows on the rocks or flagging on the trees to help you navigate this section.

Pass through the gate and follow the trail through slick-rock, mountain mahogany, and

MILEAGE/KEY POINTS	
0.0	Gate and trailhead.
0.1	Go left.
0.3	Reach a sign and veer right.
0.4	Pass through a small gate.
2.0	Reach a junction with the Broken Arrow Lookout Trail on the right; continue straight.
2.1	Veer left.
4.2	Cross a small drainage.
4.6	Steep switchbacks.
5.3	Arrive at a junction with Thompson Peak Trail. Go right, up toward the fire tower.
5.4	Arrive at the summit and fire tower.

scrub oak. Climb up a series of steep switchbacks, gaining a ridge with Glorieta Canyon on your right and Ruiz Canyon, Shaggy Peak, and Apache Canyon on your left.

Reach a junction with the Broken Arrow Lookout Trail on the right at the 2.0-mile mark. Continue straight, then stay left at a fork in the trail. The trail becomes wide and cuts through a dense ponderosa forest with views to the west and east. Level hiking is your reward for the next mile, giving you the chance to scan the ground for quartz crystals. The trail climbs and then drops down to a small drainage at the 4.2-mile mark. Cross the drainage and begin the steep grunt up to the summit. The trail, which was rerouted in 2002 to lessen the effects of erosion, switchbacks several times. Stay on the main trail and don't cut switchbacks!

After a mile of extremely steep hiking, the trail breaks out onto a sunny, south-facing hill and reaches a junction with the Thompson Peak Trail at the 5.3-mile mark. Go right and climb up to the fire tower and summit. As you look around the forested slopes of Glorieta Baldy, you'll notice that the area is far from bald. The hillsides are filled with wildflowers, and a healthy mixed-conifer forest surrounds the summit.

Views extend northeast to the Pecos Valley, south to the Ortiz Mountains and Sandia Mountains, and west to the Jemez Mountains. The fire tower is not in great condition, but the views back north to Santa Fe and the high peaks of the Pecos Wilderness are incredible from its top. Climb it at your own risk! After time spent on the summit, retrace the route back to the parking area and your car.

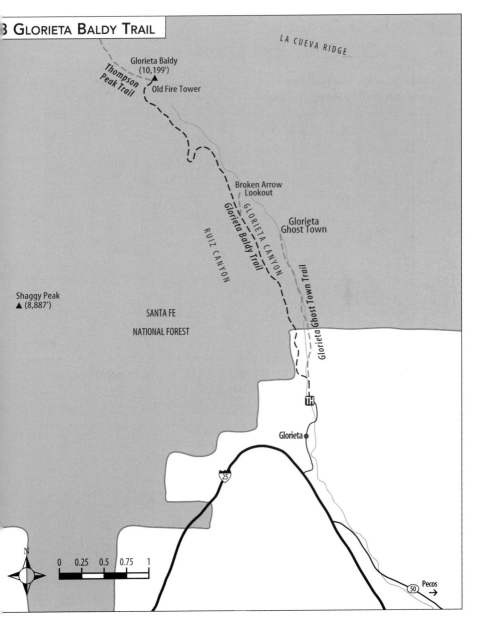

3 GLORIETA BALDY TRAIL

LA CUEVA RIDGE

Glorieta Baldy
(10,199')
Old Fire Tower

Thompson
Peak Trail

Broken Arrow
Lookout

GLORIETA CANYON

Glorieta Baldy Trail

Glorieta
Ghost Town

RUIZ CANYON

Glorieta Ghost Town Trail

Shaggy Peak
▲ (8,887')

SANTA FE

NATIONAL FOREST

TH

Glorieta ●

25

N

| 0 | 0.25 | 0.5 | 0.75 | 1 |

Pecos
→

50

HIKE 9

APACHE CANYON LOOP

HIGHLIGHTS:	Early-season wildflowers and scenic views make this convenient hike down into Apache Canyon a local favorite.
DISTANCE:	5.1-mile loop
TRAIL RATING:	Easy to moderate
HIKING TIME:	2 to 3.5 hours
LOCATION:	10 miles southeast of Santa Fe
ELEVATION:	7,700 to 8,240 feet
SEASON:	Early spring to early winter
MAPS:	Drake Mountain Maps: Mountains of Santa Fe; Santa Fe National Forest; USGS: Glorieta, McClure Reservoir
MANAGEMENT:	Santa Fe National Forest
DIRECTIONS:	From downtown Santa Fe, travel south on Old Santa Fe Trail. Stay left at its junction with Old Pecos Trail, and drive 9 miles to the village of Cañada de los Alamos, where the pavement ends. Continue 0.7 mile, turn left, travel another 0.7 mile, and turn left again. Proceed 2.8 miles (now you are on Forest Road 79) to a four-way intersection and parking area. The hike starts here.

The hike starts at the parking area and descends to the east on an old logging road. The road begins to climb, and you'll soon reach a metal gate. Pass through the gate and crest the top of a hill. Go right onto the marked Baldy Trail 175, which becomes tight and stays on a narrow ridge. Quartz crystals line the trail as it makes a quick drop down to an old logging road. Don't miss the excellent views north to the rocky summits of Shaggy Peak and Glorieta Baldy.

Go left at the road and climb gently to a trail junction at the 1.4-mile mark. Continue

MILEAGE/KEY POINTS

- 0.0 Trailhead and start of the hike.
- 0.2 Pass through a gate.
- 0.3 Go right at the sign onto Baldy Trail 175.
- 0.7 Go left on an old logging road.
- 1.4 Reach a three-way trail junction; Go left.
- 1.5 Bear right onto a narrow trail.
- 1.6 Cross the road and drop steeply into Apache Canyon.
- 1.7 Go left along Apache Creek.
- 1.8 Arrive at a trail junction and sign for Shaggy Peak (right) and Glorieta Baldy (straight). Continue straight.
- 2.0 Go left and up.
- 3.0 Go left onto the road.
- 4.0 Reach a ridgeline.
- 5.1 Back at the parking area.

straight at the junction, and within a short distance look for a narrow trail on the right at the 1.5-mile mark. Bear right and drop down to cross an old logging road. The trail drops steeply via several switchbacks to the canyon bottom and Apache Creek.

Go left at the creek and follow it upstream through several small, flower-filled meadows to a trail junction and sign at the 1.8-mile mark. (The trail leading up to the right goes to the summit of Glorieta Baldy in roughly 3 miles of steep hiking.) Continue straight along the stream and up through another resplendent meadow. At the 2.0-mile mark, go left and begin a long climb up through the ponderosas and out of Apache Canyon. Before leaving the canyon, ponder the mixed conifers along its floor and the ponderosa pines growing high on the ridge above. The presence of these trees would normally be reversed, with mixed conifers up high and ponderosa pines at lower elevations. However, the damp soil of this canyon suits spruce and fir, while ponderosa prefers the arid ridge.

After a half mile of steep ascent, the trail becomes somewhat level and slices through a nice forest of ponderosa pine. Crank up one last hill before the trail drops you onto a road. Go left and down the road, passing a small drainage. Begin to climb again, and reach a ridgeline with open views to the Jemez Mountains at the 4.0-mile mark. Pleasant hiking with nice views will bring you back to the start of the Baldy Trail. Continue down the road, pass through the gate, and head up the short hill back to your car.

9 APACHE CANYON LOOP

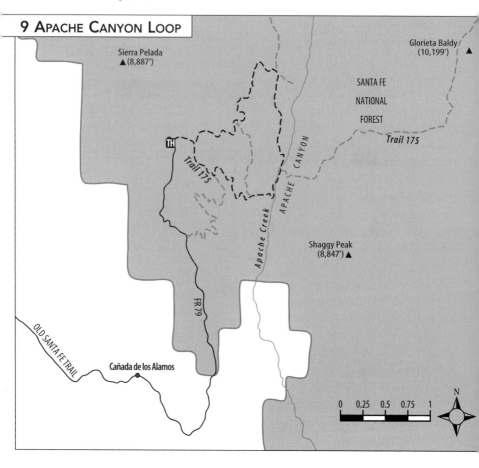

Sierra Pelada
▲ (8,887')

Glorieta Baldy
(10,199') ▲

SANTA FE

NATIONAL

FOREST

Trail 175

TH

Trail 175

FR 79

Apache Creek

APACHE CANYON

Shaggy Peak
(8,847') ▲

OLD SANTA FE TRAIL

Cañada de los Alamos

0   0.25   0.5   0.75   1

N

HIKE 10

ATALAYA MOUNTAIN

HIGHLIGHTS:	This popular route through the piñon- and juniper-studded hills to the rocky summit of Atalaya Mountain gets heavy use from hikers and mountain bikers. Try to hike mid-week for the most enjoyable journey.
DISTANCE:	3.4 miles one way
TRAIL RATING:	Moderate to strenuous
HIKING TIME:	2.5 to 3.5 hours
LOCATION:	2 miles southeast of Santa Fe
ELEVATION:	7,300 to 9,110 feet
SEASON:	Early spring to early winter
MAPS:	Drake Mountain Maps: Mountains of Santa Fe; USGS: Santa Fe
MANAGEMENT:	Santa Fe National Forest
DIRECTIONS:	From downtown Santa Fe, travel east on Alameda Street to where it bends to the right and becomes Camino Cabra. Proceed on Camino Cabra to its intersection with Camino de Cruz Blanca, and turn left and then right into St. John College. Make an immediate left into a large parking area and trailhead. The hike starts here.

Head east on Trail 174 down into Arroyo de los Chamisos. The trail hugs the edge of the arroyo and travels through stands of juniper and piñon trees, tall chamisa shrubs, and beautiful prickly pear cactus. Pass through a large, open arroyo marked with a sign to keep you on the right path. Reach a second, small arroyo, and go through a wooden gate. Reach a road at the 0.9-mile mark and cross it to the trail on the other side. This is private property (Ponderosa Estates), so stay on the trail as it climbs up through the tall pines. You'll arrive at a junction with a sign marked Trail 17 (it *should* read Trail 170) and Atalaya Mountain 2 miles. Veer right on the wide trail and begin a steep climb up through the mixed-conifer forest, passing a road on the right at the 2.3-mile mark. At the 2.6-mile mark the trail forks; take the right fork and reach another fork. Take the right fork again and enjoy some level hiking while it lasts.

MILEAGE/KEY POINTS	
0.0	Trailhead and start of the hike.
0.9	Cross the road.
1.5	Trail junction.
2.6	The trail forks; go right.
3.0	Arrive at a ridgeline and trail marker; go left.
3.4	Summit of Atalaya Mountain.

At the 2.8-mile mark, you'll arrive at the start of a series of rocky switchbacks. A steep climb will bring you to a point where the trail splits across the hill. Take the lower trail—a steep climb to a ridgeline and a sign for Trail 174. Go left along the rocky ridge through stands of Douglas fir to the summit of Atalaya Mountain.

Enjoys spectacular views down to Santa Fe, north to Apache Canyon and Glorieta Baldy, and west to the Jemez Mountains. Take a well-deserved rest before heading back down the steep trail to the trailhead.

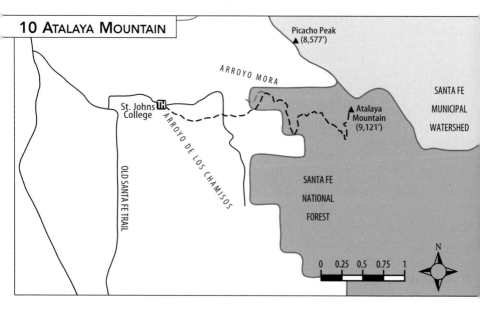

10 ATALAYA MOUNTAIN

HIKE 11

SANTA FE CANYON

Photo by Linda Montoya

Santa Fe Canyon sits below Picacho Peak and is surrounded by beautiful, rolling hills covered by piñon and juniper trees. This part of Santa Fe Canyon is protected by The Nature Conservancy, and serves as a fantastic refuge for wildlife and humans a mere 4 miles from downtown Santa Fe. Several informative kiosks along the trail highlight the wildlife, the watershed, and other important facts about this unique and lovely area.

From the parking area, pass through the gate and climb up a short hill. The trail on the right is part of the Dale Ball Trails. At the top of the hill, veer right and down along the well-worn path. Reach a bench overlooking the pond—a great place to sit for a moment. Ducks feeding in the pond may be your only company.

The trail continues down and through a thick stand of beautiful willows before it climbs to the right, reaching the breast of the old dam. Go left across the dam and then right into an open field with tall cottonwoods bordering the Santa Fe River. Go left up a short incline, and enjoy great views of Atalaya Mountain, the river valley, and south toward Santa Fe.

The trail veers right and passes through a gate. Follow it straight and then to the left, dropping steeply to Cerro Gordo Road near a small power station. Go left on the road and back to the parking area and your car.

MILEAGE/KEY POINTS
0.0 From the parking area, pass through a gate and veer left up a short hill.
0.3 Reach a bench with nice views to the pond and riparian area.
0.6 Cross over the dam and veer right.
0.7 Go left and up.
1.0 Pass through a gate.
1.3 Reach Cerro Gordo Road; go left.
1.4 Back at the parking area.

HIGHLIGHTS:	Wetlands, wildflowers, wildlife, and tall cottonwoods are the highlights of this educational, family-friendly hike in Santa Fe Canyon.
DISTANCE:	1.4-mile loop
TRAIL RATING:	Easy, with very little elevation gain
HIKING TIME:	30 minutes to an hour
LOCATION:	4 miles from downtown Santa Fe
ELEVATION:	7,300 to 7,400 feet
SEASON:	Year-round access
MAPS:	Drake Mountain Maps: Mountains of Santa Fe; USGS: McClure Reservoir
MANAGEMENT:	The Nature Conservancy
DIRECTIONS:	From downtown Santa Fe, travel east on Alameda Street to Camino Cabra. Turn right, travel a short distance, and turn left on Upper Canyon Road. Make another left at the intersection with Cerro Gordo Road. The trailhead and parking will be on your immediate right.

11 SANTA FE CANYON

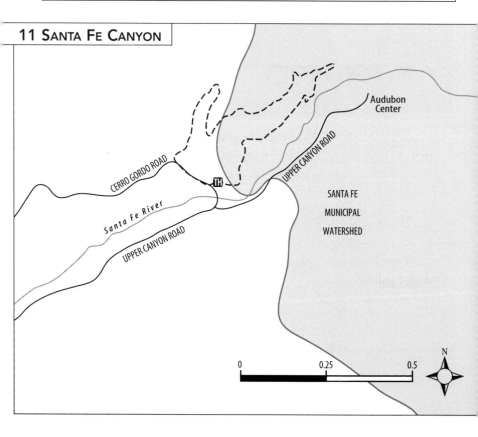

A NOTE FROM ROBERT M. FINDLING
OF THE NATURE CONSERVANCY

The Nature Conservancy's Santa Fe Canyon Preserve was established in the spring of 2000. The preserve protects a remarkable section of the Santa Fe River, which was once the heart of the Santa Fe municipal water system. The 190-acre preserve, which extends from the top of Picacho peak north toward Hyde Park Road, was the former location of the first two reservoirs that supplied Santa Fe with water. The preserve includes a short, interpretive loop trail, which explains both the natural and human history of the site.

Established on land donated by Public Service of New Mexico (PNM), the state's largest electric utility, the site protects both important wetlands and historic features. The donated parcel connects the open space lands north and south of the Santa Fe River, and allowed the construction of the adjacent Dale Ball Trails by providing essential right-of-way.

The preserve trails are only open to hiking; however, the Dale Ball Trails permit dogs and mountain bikes. For additional information call The Nature Conservancy at (505) 988-3867.

Wetlands in Santa Fe Canyon.

HIKE 12

DALE BALL TRAILS NORTH

HIGHLIGHTS:	Hikers can enjoy this easily accessible trail amid piñon- and juniper-covered hills throughout the year. This route makes a great family outing.
DISTANCE:	3.4-mile loop
TRAIL RATING:	Easy to moderate
HIKING TIME:	1 to 1.5 hours
LOCATION:	2 miles north of Santa Fe
ELEVATION:	7,700 to 7,900 feet
SEASON:	Year-round access, with some snow on the north-facing slopes during the winter months
MAPS:	Dale Ball Trails Map (can be obtained at the trailhead); Drake Mountain Maps: Mountains of Santa Fe; USGS: Santa Fe County
MANAGEMENT:	Santa Fe National Forest; County of Santa Fe; private land
DIRECTIONS:	From the intersection of Paseo de Peralta and Washington Avenue in downtown Santa Fe, travel north on Washington to Artist Road (NM 475). Turn right on Artist Road (which turns into Hyde Park Road) and travel 2.1 miles to Sierra del Norte. Turn left and make a quick right into a large parking area and the trailhead. The hike starts here.

Just 3 miles from the Plaza in downtown Santa Fe, The Dale Ball Trails are enjoyed by hikers, runners, and mountain bikers year-round. Numerous private individuals and public organizations donated time, money, land, and hard work to make

MILEAGE/KEY POINTS

0.0 Trailhead and parking area.
1.3 Bench and open views west to the Jemez Mountains.
1.7 Cross over Sierra del Norte.
1.9 Arrive at TJ3. Continue straight.
3.4 Back at the trailhead and parking area.

this system of multi-use trails available to the people of Santa Fe.

From the parking area, cross over Sierra del Norte and follow the trail (TJ9) as it begins a gentle climb and weaves through the trees. Veer left at the junction with TJ8, and climb up to a ridgeline to TJ7. Go left and then right (ignoring TJ10), and follow the trail to TJ6 and then left to TJ5. Here the route traverses the side of a west-facing hill and then drops down to Sierra del Norte.

Cross the road and pick up the trail on the other side. Climb up a short hill along a seasonal drainage to reach TJ3. Continue straight, and begin a long, gradual climb through stands of beautiful piñon and juniper trees. The trail tops out on a ridgeline with wonderful views north to

Aspen Vista and west to the Ortiz Mountains. The trail stays on the ridge for a short distance and then drops steeply back to the parking area, completing the loop.

Dale Ball Trails are for mountain bikers and hikers only.

12 DALE BALL TRAILS NORTH

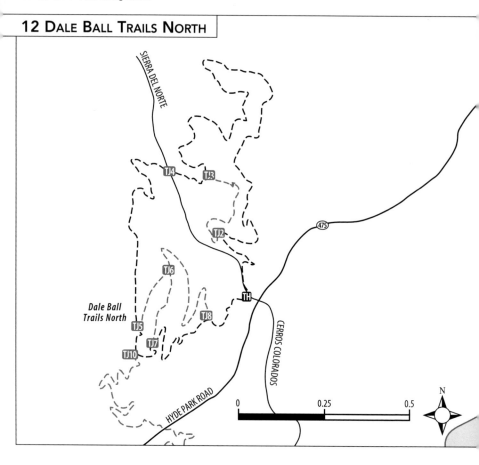

HIKE 13

CHAMISA TRAIL

Access well-marked Chamisa Trail 183 to the north and near the road. Begin a steep climb up through a heavily forested area of piñon, juniper, and ponderosa pine. Several switchbacks aid in your ascent, and the trail gains altitude at a rapid rate. As you climb higher, the vegetation changes to Gambel oak and Douglas fir. The trail becomes quite narrow and drops steeply to your left into Chamisa Canyon.

After 700 feet of elevation gain and 1.3 miles of hiking, you'll arrive at a trail junction on a saddle. The trail going left loops you back to the parking area and trailhead. Veer to the right and drop steeply down several switchbacks into a seasonal drainage. Pleasant hiking through stands of pine and aspen takes you along the drainage and into a small grass- and flower-filled meadow at the 2.0-mile mark. Wildflowers bloom profusely during the early summer months in the meadow and along the drainage. Flower lovers might want to take some short breaks and enjoy the colors. Yellow

MILEAGE/KEY POINTS

- **0.0** Trailhead and start of the hike.
- **1.3** Arrive at a saddle and trail junction; veer right.
- **2.3** Arrive Tesuque Creek, the turn-around point.
- **3.3** Continue straight on the Chamisa Trail 183. (For a different route back to the trailhead, go right.)
- **4.6** Back at the trailhead.

HIGHLIGHTS:	Close-in Chamisa Trail passes through a beautiful, narrow canyon and flower-filled meadows on its way to tumbling Tesuque Creek.
DISTANCE:	2.3 miles one way
TRAIL RATING:	Easy to moderate
HIKING TIME:	1.5 to 2.5 hours
LOCATION:	8 miles northeast of Santa Fe
ELEVATION:	7,800 to 8,440 feet
SEASON:	Early spring to early winter
MAPS:	Drake Mountain Maps: Mountains of Santa Fe; Santa Fe National Forest; USGS: Aspen Basin
MANAGEMENT:	Santa Fe National Forest
DIRECTIONS:	From the intersection of Paseo de Peralta and Washington Avenue in downtown Santa Fe, travel north on Washington to Artist Road (Hyde Park Road/NM 475). Turn right and travel 5.7 miles to the trailhead and parking area on the left. The hike starts here.

Blooming cactus along the Chamisa Trail.

evening primrose, yarrow, coneflower, and wild iris all grow in this lush meadow during the summer months.

Drop down a short distance and arrive at Tesuque Creek and a junction with the Winsor Trail in a large, grassy meadow—another great spot for wildflowers! Enjoy the meadow and Tesuque Creek before retracing your route back to the trailhead and your car.

Note: The multi-use Chamisa Trail sees a fair number of hikers and mountain bikers. Consider hiking during the week or early morning for the most enjoyable experience.

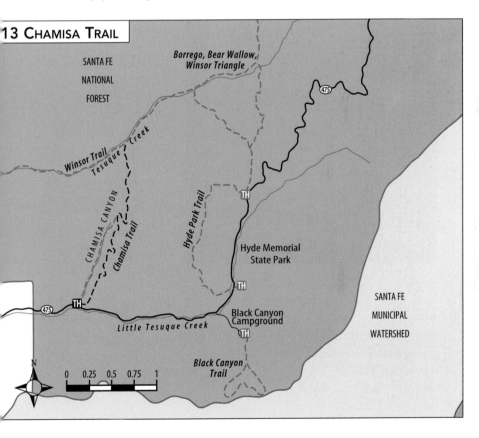

13 CHAMISA TRAIL

HIKE 14

BLACK CANYON TRAIL

This is a perfect family adventure into the woods. Parents will love the easy grade of the trail and kids will find the mileage just right for their attention spans.

Begin walking from the parking area up into the Black Canyon Campground; the road will split. Take the left fork and pass by several campsites before reaching campsite #4. For the sake of clarity, the mileage starts here. Go left, passing through the campsite and up the wide, rocky trail through a nice mixed-conifer forest.

The trail splits at a sign with arrows on it—the 0.5-mile mark. Go left and begin a short climb through a mixed-conifer forest. Keep right at the 0.8-mile mark, and continue to the top of the hill. You'll pass a sign reminding you to stay on the trail—good advice! Part of the Santa Fe watershed lies to the left of the trail and is off-limits to the public.

The trail begins to descend through a beautiful aspen forest and soon reaches a familiar junction. Continue straight down the wide trail, passing through campsite #4 again, to the trailhead and the end of the hike.

MILEAGE/KEY POINTS
0.0 Campsite #4 and the start of the mileage.
0.5 Veer left at a fork in the trail. Begin a short climb.
0.8 The trail forks; go right.
1.5 Return to a familiar junction. Continue straight and down toward campsite #4.
2.0 Reach the campsite and the hike's end.

HIGHLIGHTS:	This short, sweet hike into a small canyon near the Santa Fe watershed is a great hike for children, with wildflowers in early summer and beautiful autumn aspen.
DISTANCE:	2 miles round trip
TRAIL RATING:	Easy, with a short climb
HIKING TIME:	30 minutes to 1.5 hours
LOCATION:	8 miles northeast of Santa Fe
ELEVATION:	8,300 to 8,800 feet
SEASON:	Early spring to early winter
MAPS:	Drake Mountain Maps: Mountains of Santa Fe; USGS: McClure Reservoir.
MANAGEMENT:	Santa Fe National Forest
DIRECTIONS:	From the intersection of Paseo de Peralta and Washington Avenue in downtown Santa Fe, travel north on Washington to Artist Road (Hyde Park Road/NM 475). Turn right and travel 7 miles to the Black Canyon Campground on the right. There is day parking at the campground or along NM 475. During the summer months the campground fills quickly, and finding a parking space can be problematic. The earlier you start your hike, the better your chances of finding a place to park.

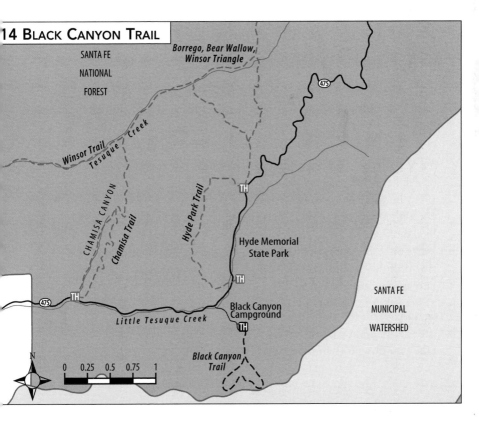

14 BLACK CANYON TRAIL

HIKE 15

HYDE PARK TRAIL

Photo by Linda Montoya

This early season hike can also be done as a loop by using trails on the north side of the highway. However, I prefer to avoid hiking along the highway and do the route as an out-and-back.

Cross the highway and go over Little Tesuque Creek via an old stone bridge. The trail veers left and then begins climbing a series of steep switchbacks, gaining elevation at a rapid rate. The route is well marked with blazes on the trees. Gain a ridge at the 0.6-mile mark, and take a short break to enjoy the views up to the ski area.

The trail now climbs at a gentle grade along the ridge with views opening across the highway to the Santa Fe watershed and Thompson Peak beyond. Continue along the ridge, hopping over several downed trees and climbing gently to the first picnic table, at the 1.6-mile mark. Look for remnants of old logging activity along the ridge and steep hillside. The second picnic table comes quickly and makes for a great spot to relax and enjoy the scenery before retracing your route back to the car.

Option: If you continue past the picnic tables, you will see a trail shooting off to the right. This is a cut-off trail that drops you quickly to the RV Park and the road. Do not take this trail, but continue straight, beginning a gradual descent down toward the road. Several trails exist on the right side of the road, and any of them will take you downhill and back to your car.

MILEAGE/KEY POINTS
0.0 Cross NM 475 and travel over Little Tesuque Creek on a stone bridge.
0.6 Reach a ridgeline.
1.6 Arrive at the first of two picnic tables.
1.8 Arrive at the second picnic table and the turnaround point.

HIGHLIGHTS:	This trail offers almost year-round access and great views of the surrounding mountains and the city of Santa Fe.
DISTANCE:	1.8 miles one way
TRAIL RATING:	Moderate, with a steep climb at the start
HIKING TIME:	1.5 to 2.5 hours
LOCATION:	8 miles northeast of Santa Fe
ELEVATION:	8,400 to 9,400 feet
SEASON:	Early spring to early winter
MAPS:	Drake Mountain Maps: Mountains of Santa Fe; Santa Fe National Forest; USGS: McClure Reservoir
MANAGEMENT:	Santa Fe National Forest
DIRECTIONS:	From the intersection of Paseo de Peralta and Washington Avenue in downtown Santa Fe, travel north on Washington to Artist Road (Hyde Park Road/NM 475). Turn right and travel 7.4 miles to the Hyde Memorial State Park. Parking is on the right near the store.

15 HYDE PARK TRAIL

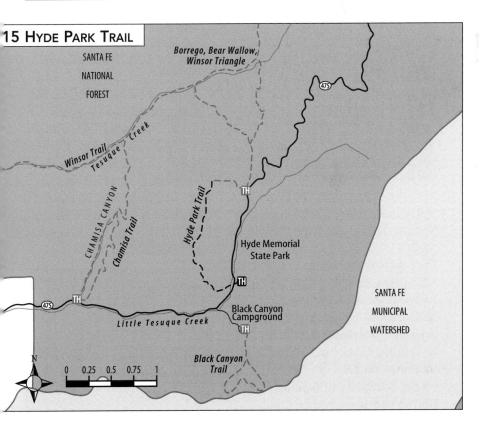

HIKE 16

BORREGO, BEAR WALLOW, WINSOR TRIANGLE

Photo by Mike Butterfield

Herders bringing their animals from the north to the market in Santa Fe used the Borrego (sheep) Trail. The trail is well worn and sees a tremendous amount of activity on weekends during the summer months. For those of you who cherish solitude, hike the trail in the early morning or on weekdays.

Access the start of the trail at the far end of the parking area. A sign reads Borrego Trail 150. Follow the trail down into a dense conifer forest descending over waterbars and rocks. After an easy half-mile of hiking, you'll arrive at a trail junction. Go left on the Bear Wallow Trail and descend on the now narrow path along the Bear Wallow drainage. You will cross the drainage several times before reaching a short, steep uphill at the 1.0-mile mark. Climb up the narrow, exposed trail, bear right at the top of the hill, and drop down on two steep switchbacks to Tesuque Creek.

Cross the creek and go right on the Winsor Trail, heading up canyon and through a beautiful, small meadow. At the far end of the meadow, you'll begin a

MILEAGE/KEY POINTS
0.0 Trailhead and start of the hike.
0.4 Reach a trail junction; go left.
1.0 Short, steep climb.
1.4 Cross Tesuque Creek and arrive at the Winsor Trail; go right.
2.2 Reach the Borrego Trail.
2.3 Cross Tesuque Creek via a large log.
3.0 Reach a saddle.
3.3 Arrive back at the Bear Wallow Trail.
3.7 Back at the parking area.

HIGHLIGHTS:	This hike close to Santa Fe is a great introduction to wonderful trails along NM 475 near the Big Tesuque drainage.
DISTANCE:	3.7 miles round trip
TRAIL RATING:	Easy to moderate
HIKING TIME:	1 to 2 hours
LOCATION:	8 miles northeast of Santa Fe
ELEVATION:	8,200 to 8,840 feet
SEASON:	Early spring to early winter
MAPS:	Drake Mountain Maps: Mountains of Santa Fe; Santa Fe National Forest; USGS: Aspen Basin
MANAGEMENT:	Santa Fe National Forest
DIRECTIONS:	From the intersection of Paseo de Peralta and Washington Avenue in downtown Santa Fe, travel north on Washington to Artist Road (Hyde Park Road/NM 475). Turn right and travel 8.5 miles to the trailhead and parking area on the left. The hike starts here.

long, moderate climb along Tesuque Creek to a junction with the Borrego Trail at the 2.2-mile mark. Go right across the creek on a large log, and drop gently along the drainage to the start of several steep switchbacks at the 2.5-mile mark. Begin a steep climb up the switchbacks on a narrow trail that pulls away from the drainage through a dense conifer forest before reaching a saddle at the 3.0-mile mark. The trail makes a sudden drop on the other side of the saddle and quickly delivers you back to a familiar trail junction. Continue heading straight, and climb gently to the trailhead and your car.

16 Borrego, Bear Wallow, Winsor Triangle

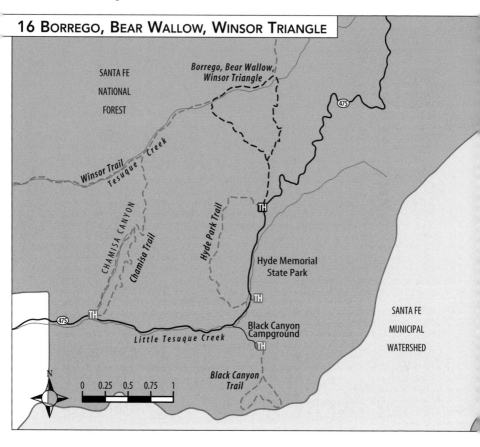

Hike 17

Aspen Vista

Photo by Linda Montoya

Highlights:	Beautiful wildflowers in the summer months and the changing aspen in the autumn accent this excursion to the summit of 12,042-foot Tesuque Peak.
Distance:	6 miles one way
Trail Rating:	Moderate, with a long, gradual climb to Tesuque Peak
Hiking Time:	4 to 7 hours
Location:	15 miles northeast of Santa Fe
Elevation:	10,000 to 12,040 feet
Season:	Early June to late October
Maps:	Drake Mountain Maps: Mountains of Santa Fe; Santa Fe National Forest; USGS: Aspen Basin
Management:	Santa Fe National Forest
Directions:	From the intersection of Paseo de Peralta and Washington Avenue in downtown Santa Fe, head north on Washington to Artist Road (Hyde Park Road/NM 475). Turn right and travel 12.6 miles to the trailhead and parking area on the right. The hike starts here.

This is a popular fall hike when the aspen trees are changing colors. Be sure to bring proper clothing and enough food and water for this long hike at altitude. Snow can remain on the upper slopes well into July, and the weather can change rapidly and without warning at 12,000 feet, so be prepared!

Pass through the gate and begin walking up Forest Road 150. The road climbs at a gentle grade through a large aspen forest before it swings to the east and crosses the North Fork of Tesuque Creek at the 0.8-mile mark. Water-loving flowers grow along the banks of the creek during the mid-summer months. Tesuque Peak is straight ahead, with micro towers sprouting from its bald summit—your destination! Make three more stream-crossings. The road switchbacks to the north at the 3.2-mile mark and enters mixed-conifer forest before it traverses across a large, open meadow with open views to the right at 3.7 miles.

Feeling the effects of the altitude yet? The trail is now 11,000 feet above sea level. Hiking becomes steeper through this section as views open down to Santa Fe. Climb past several switchbacks and enter mixed-conifer forest again. The road climbs quickly and enters a large alpine meadow at the 5.4-mile mark. This is a good spot for a short break to enjoy the wildflowers and the views of the Santa Fe Ski Basin on the left and the Santa Fe Mountains on the right.

The road passes through a break in the fence line at the 5.6-mile mark, veers to the right, and circles back south to the summit of Tesuque Peak at 6.0 miles. There are great views north out to Lake Peak and Penitente Peak and down to Santa Fe Lake. This lake is a source of water for the city of Santa Fe and part of the Santa Fe Watershed. Enjoy your time on the summit before retracing the route back to the trailhead and your car.

MILEAGE/KEY POINTS

0.0 Begin climbing on Aspen Vista Road/FR 150.

0.8 Cross the North Fork of Tesuque Creek.

1.8 Cross two small streams.

2.6 Cross over a branch of Tesuque Creek.

3.7 Reach a large open meadow.

5.4 Enter a high-alpine meadow.

5.6 Pass through a break in the wooden fence line.

6.0 Reach the summit of Tesuque Peak.

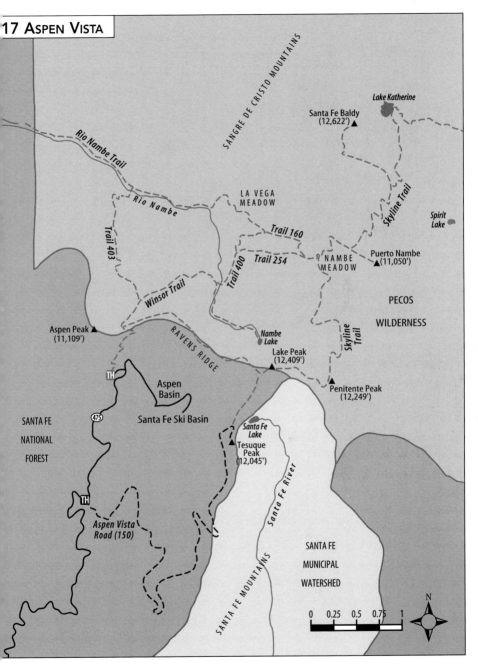

17 ASPEN VISTA

SANGRE DE CRISTO MOUNTAINS

Lake Katherine

Santa Fe Baldy
(12,622')

Rio Nambe Trail

Skyline Trail

Spirit
Lake

LA VEGA
MEADOW

Rio Nambe

Trail 160

Trail 403

Trail 400

Trail 254

NAMBE
MEADOW

Puerto Nambe
(11,050')

PECOS

WILDERSHESS

Winsor Trail

Skyline
Trail

Aspen Peak
(11,109')

RAVENS RIDGE

Nambe
Lake

Lake Peak
(12,409')

TH

Aspen
Basin

Penitente Peak
(12,249')

475

Santa Fe Ski Basin

Santa Fe
Lake

SANTA FE

NATIONAL

FOREST

Tesuque
Peak
(12,045')

TH

Aspen Vista
Road (150)

Santa Fe River

SANTA FE

MUNICIPAL

WATERSHED

SANTA FE MOUNTAINS

N

0   0.25   0.5   0.75   1

HIKE 18

LAKE PEAK

HIGHLIGHTS:	Although this hike to the rocky and rugged summit of Lake Peak is strenuous, the spectacular views along the ridge and panoramic views from the top are well worth the work!
DISTANCE:	3.2 miles one way
TRAIL RATING:	Difficult
HIKING TIME:	3 to 6 hours
LOCATION:	15 miles northeast of Santa Fe
ELEVATION:	10,200 to 12,400 feet
SEASON:	Early June to late October
MAPS:	Drake Mountain Maps: Mountains of Santa Fe; Santa Fe National Forest; USGS: Aspen Basin.
MANAGEMENT:	Santa Fe National Forest
DIRECTIONS:	From downtown Santa Fe, access NM 475 (Artist Road/Hyde Park Road) and travel 15 miles to the Santa Fe Ski Basin and a large parking area on the left. The trailhead is well marked and starts near the bathrooms.

9/04   nice hike w/ views
golden aspens

This route links three trails as it leads to the summit of Lake Peak. Start the hike by accessing the Winsor Trail from Santa Fe Ski Basin's upper parking area near a kiosk and the bathrooms. Cross the bridge, turn right on the marked Winsor Trail 254, and head north toward Aspen Peak. The trail climbs up several

MILEAGE/KEY POINTS	
0.0	Parking area and trailhead.
0.5	Reach a fence line and the boundary of the Pecos Wilderness. Go right, up along the fence.
1.2	Reach an overlook.
1.7	Trail junction. Go left.
2.8	Reach a junction with the Skyline Trail.
3 2	Summit of Lake Peak.

long, steep switchbacks in a dense, mixed-conifer forest, past several signs asking you not to cut switchbacks. It is very important to stay on the trail here in order to prevent erosion.

After a half-mile of steep hiking and 600 feet of elevation gain, you will reach a saddle, a gate, and the boundary for the Pecos Wilderness. The shaded forest up to the gate is the perfect environment for the fairy slipper orchid, a delicate little gem that blooms in June. Look for the Ravens Ridge Trail on the right, just before the gate, and take it to the right. You'll begin a steep climb up the ridge, following the fence line through a forest of pine and aspen. At approximately the 1-mile mark, you'll reach an open meadow with good views and blooming wildflowers during the summer months. An abrupt turn to the right lands you on the narrow ridgeline at a rocky overlook with spectacular views to Santa Fe Baldy, Lake Peak, and down to the Rio Nambe. This is a great spot to stop and relax.

The next half-mile is extremely steep, and the trail stays to the left, passing beside two talus slopes. At the top of the second talus slope, follow the trail through the trees and up to a junction. Go left into a forest of tall pines, back toward the ridge, and then down. You'll see a trail shooting down and right and back to the ski area, but continue straight and up to where the trail breaks out into the open tundra. Climb steeply up to the obvious ridgeline, which leads north to Lake Peak and the Skyline Trail.

From this point there are great views in all directions. I saw several large, noisy ravens on the ridge and can see how this beautiful place got its name! Follow the Skyline Trail north as it hugs and clings to the narrow ridge. Stay on the east side of the ridge, and carefully skirt the exposed, rocky sections. After hiking about one-third of a mile on the ridge, you will reach the impressive summit of Lake Peak. Spectacular views to the Jemez Mountains, Santa Fe Baldy, the high peaks of the Pecos Wilderness, and east down to Nambe Lake will take your breath away (if the altitude hasn't already done so).

18 LAKE PEAK

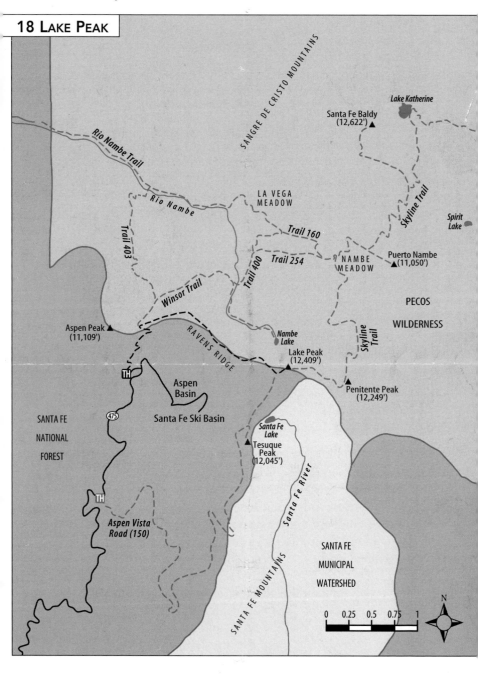

SANGRE DE CRISTO MOUNTAINS

Lake Katherine

Santa Fe Baldy
(12,622')

Rio Nambe Trail

Rio Nambe

LA VEGA
MEADOW

Trail 160

Skyline Trail

Spirit
Lake

Trail 403

Trail 400

Trail 254

NAMBE
MEADOW

Puerto Nambe
(11,050')

PECOS

Winsor Trail

Aspen Peak
(11,109')

RAVENS RIDGE

Nambe
Lake

Lake Peak
(12,409')

Skyline
Trail

WILDERNESS

TH

Aspen
Basin

475

Santa Fe Ski Basin

Penitente Peak
(12,249')

SANTA FE

NATIONAL

FOREST

Santa Fe
Lake

Tesuque
Peak
(12,045')

Santa Fe River

TH

Aspen Vista
Road (150)

SANTA FE

MUNICIPAL

WATERSHED

SANTA FE MOUNTAINS

N

0   0.25   0.5   0.75   1

NAMBE LAKE

This hike starts at the trailhead near the kiosk and bathrooms at the upper parking area of the Santa Fe Ski Basin. Cross the bridge and turn right on the marked Winsor Trail 254, heading north toward Aspen Peak. The trail climbs steeply up several long switchbacks through a dense, mixed-confer forest. You will pass several signs telling you not to cut switchbacks—don't! After a half-mile of steep hiking and 600 feet of elevation gain, you will reach a saddle, a gate, and the boundary for the Pecos Wilderness. (You'll see the Ravens Ridge Trail, which climbs steeply to Lake Peak, just to the right along the gate.) Continue straight through the gate, and begin a gentle descent through the dense forest on a wide, sometimes rocky, trail.

You'll reach a junction with the Rio Nambe Trail at mile 0.7. (This trail drops steeply for a little less than 2 miles to the Rio Nambe and is nicknamed "The Elevator Shaft" for its steep nature and lack of switchbacks.) Continue straight on the Winsor Trail as it cuts through a stand of tall, stately aspen around the 1.5-mile mark. This section is quite spectacular when the leaves change in late September and early October.

MILEAGE/KEY POINTS
0.0 Parking area and trailhead.
0.5 Boundary of the Pecos Wilderness.
0.7 Rio Nambe Trail on the left.
1.8 Junction with the Nambe Trail 400; go right.
3.4 Arrive at Nambe Lake.

HIGHLIGHTS:	Nambe Lake, nestled tightly below Lake Peak in a spectacular rocky cirque, makes a great destination for an alpine hike, particularly at peak-wildflower and peak-leaf times.
DISTANCE:	3.4 miles one way
TRAIL RATING:	Difficult
HIKING TIME:	3 to 6 hours
LOCATION:	15 miles northeast of Santa Fe
ELEVATION:	10,260 to 11,400 feet
SEASON:	Early June to late October
MAPS:	Drake Mountain Maps: Mountains of Santa Fe; Santa Fe National Forest; USGS: Aspen Basin
MANAGEMENT:	Santa Fe National Forest
DIRECTIONS:	From downtown Santa Fe, access NM 475 (Artist Road/ Hyde Park Road) and travel 15 miles to the Santa Fe Ski Basin and a large parking area on the right. The trailhead is well marked and starts near the bathrooms.

You'll see the Nambe Trail 400 heading off to the right near the 1.8-mile mark. Go right on Nambe Trail, and climb up to a small meadow filled with wildflowers during the summer months. The wild-flowing Rio Nambe will be on your left. Numerous trails shoot out in various directions, which can be quite confusing. Take the trail nearest the stream, climbing steeply to a crossing. Go left, over the stream, and climb away from the water. The trail then contours back to the stream and climbs very steeply up to a large, beautiful, wildflower-filled meadow on the right. Be on the lookout for tall chiming bells, columbine, golden banner, and paintbrush. The meadow on the right holds thousands of pink elephant heads (flowers, not pachyderms) during the months of July and August.

The trail becomes quite rough after it passes through the meadow, and you'll begin to see numerous rock walls to the left of the stream. The landscape takes on an alpine appearance as you draw near to Nambe Lake. The rocky summit of Lake Peak towers above the water to the east, and Ravens Ridge is to the west, with the Santa Fe Ski Basin beyond it.

A trail skirts the lake, with several spots to relax, eat lunch, and take in the panoramic views. If you follow the trail just left of the lake, you'll soon see the Rio Nambe. You can follow the stream up to its source at a large talus slope, which is also a nice place to relax and to replenish your water supply. (Remember to filter or treat the water before drinking it!) When you are ready to leave this peaceful place, retrace the route back to the trailhead.

19 NAMBE LAKE

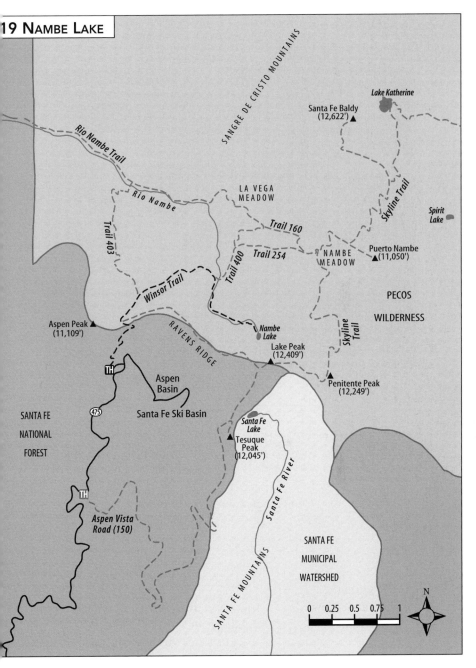

Lake Katherine

Santa Fe Baldy
(12,622')

Skyline Trail

Spirit Lake

SANGRE DE CRISTO MOUNTAINS

Rio Nambe Trail

Rio Nambe

LA VEGA MEADOW

Trail 160

Trail 403

Trail 400

Trail 254

NAMBE MEADOW

Puerto Nambe
(11,050')

PECOS

WILDERNESS

Winsor Trail

Aspen Peak
(11,109')

RAVENS RIDGE

Nambe Lake

Lake Peak
(12,409')

Skyline Trail

TH

Aspen Basin

Santa Fe Ski Basin

Penitente Peak
(12,249')

SANTA FE

NATIONAL

FOREST

475

Santa Fe Lake

Tesuque Peak
(12,045')

TH

Aspen Vista Road (150)

Santa Fe River

SANTA FE

MUNICIPAL

WATERSHED

SANTA FE MOUNTAINS

N

0   0.25   0.5   0.75   1

HIKE 20

PUERTO NAMBE

HIGHLIGHTS:	Wildflowers flourishing in the alpine meadows and expansive views of Santa Fe Baldy, Lake Peak, and Penitente Peak contribute to the splendor of this challenging hike.
DISTANCE:	4.0 miles one way
TRAIL RATING:	Difficult
HIKING TIME:	3 to 6 hours
LOCATION:	15 miles northeast of Santa Fe
ELEVATION:	10,260 to 11,100 feet
SEASON:	Mid-June to late October
MAPS:	Drake Mountain Maps: Mountains of Santa Fe; Santa Fe National Forest; USGS: Aspen Basin
MANAGEMENT:	Santa Fe National Forest
DIRECTIONS:	From downtown Santa Fe, take NM 475 (Artist Road/Hyde Park Road) 15 miles to the Santa Fe Ski Basin and a large parking area on the right. The trailhead is well marked and starts near the bathrooms.

This hike also starts on the Winsor Trail. Access it near the kiosk and bathrooms at the upper parking area of the Santa Fe Ski Basin. Cross the bridge and turn right on the marked Winsor Trail 254, heading north toward Aspen Peak. The trail climbs up several steep,

MILEAGE/ KEY POINTS

0.0 Parking area and trailhead.
0.5 Boundary of the Pecos Wilderness.
0.7 Rio Nambe Trail on the left.
1.8 Junction with the Nambe Trail 400; continue straight.
3.0 Junction with Rio the Nambe Trail 160; continue straight.
4.0 Arrive at Puerto Nambe Meadow.

long switchbacks (with signs asking you not to short-cut them) through a dense, mixed-confer forest.

Roughly a half-mile of steep hiking and 600 feet of elevation gain will bring you to a saddle, a gate, and the boundary for the Pecos Wilderness. Keep an eye out for the fairy slipper orchid here in June. (You'll see Ravens Ridge Trail on the right along the gate.) Continue straight through the gate, and begin a gentle but rocky descent through the dense forest on a wide trail. At the 0.7-mile mark, you'll reach a junction with the Rio Nambe Trail. Continue straight on the Winsor Trail. You'll soon enter a stand of aspen at approximately 1.5 miles.

Around the 1.8-mile mark, you'll reach a trail marked Nambe Trail 400 going off to the right. Continue straight and down, crossing the Rio Nambe. This section of the trail can be extremely wet during the early summer months. Shortly after the creek crossing, you'll arrive at a marked junction where the Rio Nambe Trail 160 goes up and left to La Vega. Continue on the Winsor Trail and cross over two small drainages before climbing a series of steep switchbacks to Puerto Nambe Meadow. Proceed through the grassy meadow to reach a junction with Skyline Trail 251 and the turnaround point.

This meadow is a great spot to relax, take in the incredible views, and look at the variety of wildflowers that bloom in the midsummer months. After your rest, retrace your route back to the trailhead and the parking area.

20 PUERTO NAMBE

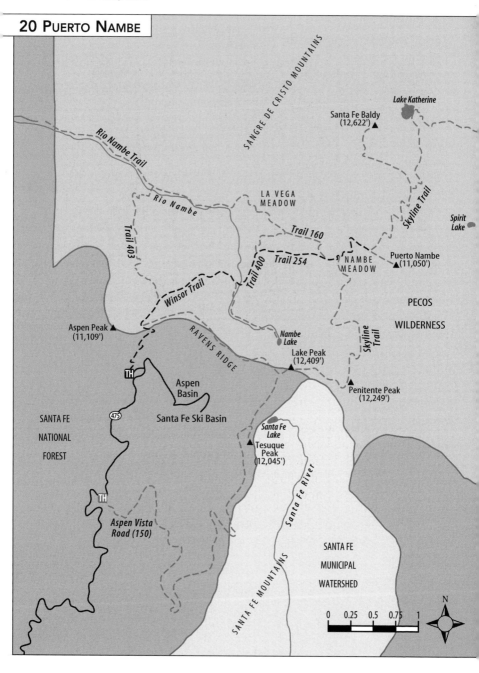

SANGRE DE CRISTO MOUNTAINS

Lake Katherine

Santa Fe Baldy
(12,622') ▲

Río Nambe Trail

Río Nambe

Skyline Trail

Spirit
Lake

LA VEGA
MEADOW

Trail 160

Trail 403

Trail 400

Trail 254

NAMBE
MEADOW

Puerto Nambe
▲(11,050')

Winsor Trail

PECOS

WILDERNESS

Aspen Peak ▲
(11,109')

RAVENS RIDGE

Nambe
Lake

Skyline
Trail

TH

Lake Peak
(12,409') ▲

Aspen
Basin

Penitente Peak
(12,249') ▲

475

Santa Fe Ski Basin

Santa Fe
Lake

SANTA FE

NATIONAL

FOREST

Tesuque
Peak
(12,045') ▲

Santa Fe River

TH

Aspen Vista
Road (150)

SANTA FE
MOUNTAINS

SANTA FE

MUNICIPAL

WATERSHED

N

0   0.25   0.5   0.75   1

HIKE 21

LA VEGA

This hike follows the Winsor Trail 254 for a few miles before going left on the La Vega Shortcut Trail. Start by accessing the Winsor Trail from the upper parking area of the Santa Fe Ski Basin. The trailhead is near a kiosk and the bathrooms.

Cross the bridge and turn right on the marked Winsor Trail 254, heading north toward Aspen Peak. The trail climbs up several long switchbacks in a dense conifer forest. You'll pass several signs telling you not to cut switchbacks—please don't! After a half-mile of steep hiking and 600 feet of elevation gain, you will reach a saddle, a gate, and the boundary for the Pecos Wilderness. Scan the shady spots for the fairy slipper orchid, a delicate little flower that blooms here in June. You'll see Ravens Ridge Trail off to the right along the gate, but continue straight and begin a gentle descent through the dense forest on a wide, sometimes rocky trail.

At the 0.7-mile mark, you'll reach a junction with the Rio Nambe Trail 403. This trail, which drops steeply for just under 2 miles to the river, deserves its nickname: The

MILEAGE/KEY POINTS	
0.0	Parking area and trailhead.
0.5	Boundary of the Pecos Wilderness.
0.7	Rio Nambe Trail 403 on the left.
1.8	Junction with the Nambe Trail 400; continue straight.
2.4	Upper Nambe Trail 101; go left.
3.0	Rio Nambe Trail 160; go left.
3.3	La Vega Meadow.

HIGHLIGHTS:	Lovely wildflowers, dense stands of aspen, and staggering views of Santa Fe Baldy accent this hike to one of the most beautiful meadows in the southern Sangre de Cristo Mountains.
DISTANCE:	3.3 miles one way
TRAIL RATING:	Moderate
HIKING TIME:	3 to 6 hours
LOCATION:	15 miles northeast of Santa Fe
ELEVATION:	10,260 to 10,840 feet
SEASON:	Mid-June to late October
MAPS:	Santa Fe National Forest; USGS: Aspen Basin
MANAGEMENT:	Santa Fe National Forest
DIRECTIONS:	From downtown Santa Fe, access NM 475 (Artist Road/ Hyde Park Road) and travel 15 miles to the Santa Fe Ski Basin and a large parking lot on the right. The well-marked trailhead is near the bathrooms.

Elevator Shaft. Continue straight on the Winsor Trail. Around the 1.5-mile mark, the trail cuts through a stand of tall, stately aspen—particularly spectacular in late September and early October, when the leaves change.

You'll reach a trail marked Nambe Trail 400 going off to the right near the 1.8-mile mark. (This trail leads on a steep ascent along the Rio Nambe up to beautiful Nambe Lake.) Continue straight and down through an open area, and cross the Rio Nambe. This section of the trail can be extremely wet during the early summer months. A short distance after the creek crossing, you'll arrive at a junction at the 2.4-mile mark, indicating Upper Nambe Trail 101 and La Vega. Go left and begin a pleasant downhill through the forest and into a grassy meadow filled with aspen. From here, the trail drops down and crosses the Rio Nambe via logs before veering uphill to the left and away from the river.

When you reach a junction with the Rio Nambe Trail 160 at the 3.0-mile mark, go left, following the narrow and rocky trail down and then up to a small clearing with a sign for La Vega. Continue heading straight, and arrive at a large, open meadow nestled below the towering west flank of Santa Fe Baldy. La Vega Meadow is a wildflower-lover's dream, filled with bright blossoms from mid-June to mid-August. Enjoy the meadow before retracing your route back to the trailhead and your car.

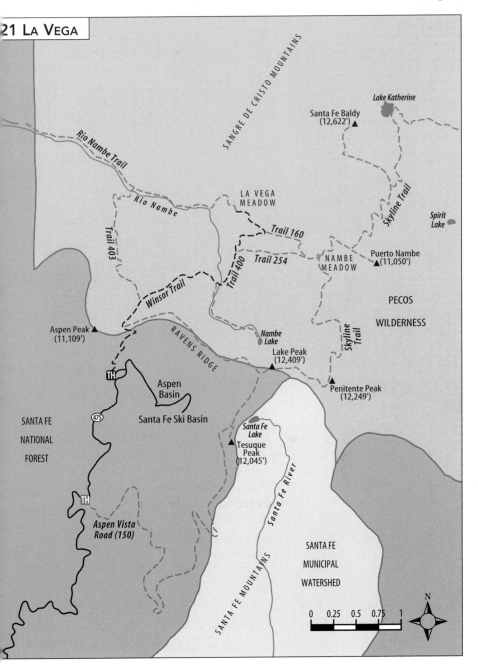

21 LA VEGA

HIKE 22

SANTA FE BALDY

HIGHLIGHTS:	Panoramic views, beautiful wildflowers, cool mountain streams, open alpine meadows, and a true summit for the peak-bagger await you on this long, strenuous day hike up to the highest point near Santa Fe.
DISTANCE:	6.8 miles one way
TRAIL RATING:	Difficult
HIKING TIME:	5 to 10 hours
LOCATION:	15 miles northeast of Santa Fe
ELEVATION:	10,260 to 12,620 feet
SEASON:	Mid-June to late October
MAPS:	Drake Mountain Maps: Mountains of Santa Fe; Santa Fe National Forest; USGS: Aspen Basin
MANAGEMENT:	Santa Fe National Forest
DIRECTIONS:	From downtown Santa Fe, access NM 475 (Artist Road/ Hyde Park Road) and travel 15 miles to the Santa Fe Ski Basin and a large parking area on the right. The well-marked trailhead is near the bathrooms.

This is a long and arduous hike up to the towering summit of Santa Fe Baldy. Those attempting this route should be in excellent physical shape and able to hike at altitude.

Start the hike by accessing the Winsor Trail from the upper parking area of the Santa Fe Ski Basin. The trailhead is near a kiosk and the bathrooms. Cross the bridge and turn right on the

MILEAGE/KEY POINTS
0.0 Parking area and trailhead.
0.5 Boundary of the Pecos Wilderness.
0.7 Rio Nambe Trail on the left.
1.8 Junction with the Nambe Trail 400; continue straight.
3.0 Junction with the Rio Nambe Trail 160; continue straight.
4.2 Arrive at Nambe Meadow. Go left on the Skyline Trail 251.
5.6 Reach the ridgeline.
6.8 Summit of Santa Fe Baldy.

Winsor Trail 254 heading north toward Aspen Peak. You will pass several signs asking you not to cut the switchbacks as the trail climbs steeply in a dense forest of mixed confers.

After 0.5 mile of steep hiking and 600 feet of elevation gain, you will reach a saddle, a gate, and the boundary for the Pecos Wilderness. (The Ravens Ridge Trail shoots to the right along the gate and climbs steeply toward Lake Peak.) Continue straight through the gate, and begin a gentle descent through dense forest on a wide, rough trail. You will reach a junction with the Rio Nambe Trail at the 0.7-mile mark. (This trail drops steeply for a little under 2 miles to the Rio Nambe and is nicknamed "The Elevator Shaft" for its plunging nature and lack of switchbacks.) Continue straight on the Winsor Trail. Near the 1.5-mile mark, the trail cuts through a stand of tall, stately aspens

Around the 1.8-mile mark, you'll reach a trail marked Nambe Trail 400, which goes off to the right. Continue straight and down to cross the Rio Nambe. This section of the trail can be extremely wet during the early summer months, but offers nice hiking through a lovely mixed-conifer forest. A short distance after the creek crossing, you arrive at a junction with the marked Rio Nambe Trail 160 going up and left to La Vega. Continue on the Winsor Trail, cross over two small drainages, and begin climbing a series of steep switchbacks to the Puerto Nambe Meadow. Continue though the grassy meadow to the junction with Skyline Trail 251. If you've been keeping a good pace, and have a few minutes to spare, this is a great spot to take a short rest before tackling the steep terrain ahead.

Follow the Skyline Trail as it heads toward Lake Katherine, climbing steeply and gaining the crest of a high ridge. Once on the ridge, you have a few decisions to make. The rest of this hike follows the exposed ridge up to the summit of Santa Fe Baldy. This ridgeline is prone to lightning strikes and is not a safe place to be during turbulent weather. If the sky looks the least bit threatening, you might want to change your plans and head back to the trailhead. You will also gain a staggering 1,000 feet in just over a mile of climbing from this point to the summit. If you are feeling the negative effects of altitude, this is a good turnaround point.

However, if the skies are smiling and you feel good, turn left and leave the trail, following the steep ridge to the impressive summit of 12,622-foot Santa Fe Baldy. You may encounter small patches of snow along the ridge as late as August. Impressive views from the peak stretch in all directions, and you can walk a short distance to the northeast for a particularly great view of Lake Katherine. Enjoy your time on the summit, then retrace your route back to the trailhead and your car.

Pleasant hiking through tall pines.

22 SANTA FE BALDY

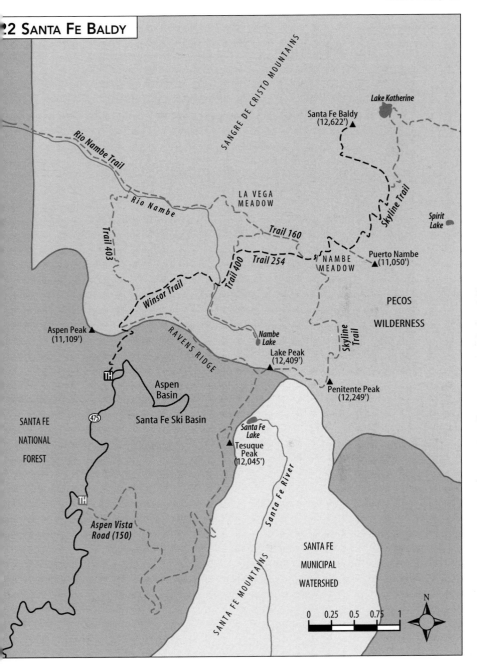

HIKE 23

RIO EN MEDIO

HIGHLIGHTS:	This wonderful and rugged hike takes you through a narrow canyon along the Rio en Medio, past towering rock walls and cascading waterfalls, to a beautiful open meadow near Aspen Park. It's one of the best late-spring hikes in the Santa Fe area!
DISTANCE:	4.0 miles one way
TRAIL RATING:	Strenuous, due to a big climb and elevation gain
HIKING TIME:	3 to 6 hours
LOCATION:	15 miles north of Santa Fe
ELEVATION:	7,300 to 8,900 feet
SEASON:	Late spring to late fall
MAPS:	Drake Mountain Maps: Mountains of Santa Fe; USGS: Aspen Basin
MANAGEMENT:	Santa Fe National Forest
DIRECTIONS:	From Santa Fe, travel north on US 84 for 8 miles to Tesuque. Turn right at the light. Make a quick right onto NM 592 and proceed 6.5 miles to the small village of En Medio. Follow the road to a small parking area and the trailhead marked by a Forest Service sign on the right. The hike starts here.

Follow the road east from the parking area toward a private residence. Go right onto a narrow trail that parallels a fence. The trail stays close to the Rio en Medio and then crosses it at the 0.4-mile mark. Pass by a cluster of prickly pear cacti and begin a gradual climb up the narrow canyon. The trail climbs at a modest rate and crosses the Rio en Medio via rocks and logs several times. Tall, beautiful Douglas firs and ponderosa pines line the trail, and wild-

MILEAGE/KEY POINTS	
0.0	Trailhead/parking.
0.1	Go right onto a narrow trail along a fence line.
0.4	Cross the Rio en Medio.
0.7	Cross the creek again.
1.2	Arrive at a trail junction in a small meadow; continue straight.
1.7	Spectacular waterfall on the left.
2.0	Towering rock wall on the left, cascading waterfall on the right.
2.5	Switchbacks begin.
2.7	Reach a saddle.
3.5	Large, open meadow.
4.0	Arrive at a junction with Trail 160.

flowers grow in the moist soil near the trail. Reach a trail junction at the 1.2-mile mark. Continue straight through the open meadow, staying to the right, then heading left over the stream. The trail begins to climb through a very narrow canyon. At the 1.7-mile mark, you'll see a spectacular waterfall on the left. To get a better view of the falls, cross the stream and scramble onto the rock perch.

Backtrack to the main trail and climb up a steep rocky section gaining a small shelf. The trail crosses the stream and passes by a towering rock to your left. Look right to the stream and a long ribbon of small water-falls—a very beautiful spot! The trail crosses the stream and then begins to climb away from the drainage via very steep and rocky switchbacks. At the top of the climb, look downstream for great views of the rock wall and beyond.

The trail veers right, and pleasant hiking is the norm for the next mile. Cross the stream once more, and then pass a beautiful meadow at the 3.5-mile mark. Continue straight through the trees, and you'll arrive at the junction with Trail 160 and the turnaround point. Retrace the route back to your car and the trailhead.

23 RIO EN MEDIO

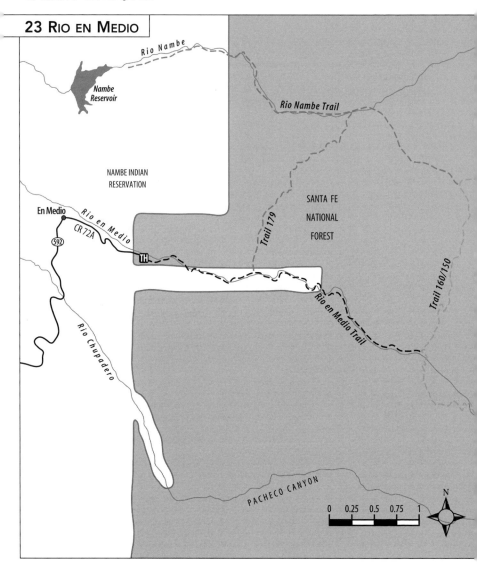

TESUQUE CREEK

The hike offers lovely scenery: deep, green forests; colorful wildflowers; and a chance to get into the woods close to the city. The well-used trail sees heavy foot- and mountain-bike traffic during weekends in the summer months. To enjoy some solitude, do the hike midweek or early in the morning.

From the parking area, head east on CR 72A, and look for signs marking the Winsor Trail. Bear right at 0.2 mile and cross a footbridge over Tesuque Creek. Stay on the trail through private property as it parallels a fence and the creek. You'll reach an intersection at the 0.6-mile mark; continue straight. (The road going right leads to Bishops Lodge, and the road going left is private.) Pass through a beautiful riparian area with tall cottonwood trees and thick willows. Bear right over the bridge and reach the boundary of the Santa Fe National Forest at a gate and sign.

Several trail options exist here. For this hike, cross the stream to reach a wide, rocky road on the right side of the

MILEAGE/KEY POINTS	
0.0	Head east on CR 72A.
0.2	Bear right and cross a footbridge.
0.6	Continue straight at an intersection.
0.9	Gate and boundary of the Santa Fe National Forest.
1.1	Junction with the Juan Trail; bear left.
1.4	The first of several creek crossings.
3.2	The last of the creek crossings.
3.7	Arrive at a beautiful meadow and a junction with the Chamisa Trail.

HIGHLIGHTS:	This short, easy-to-access hike up a beautiful canyon and along the lovely Tesuque Creek can be enjoyed virtually year round, though the wildflowers and fresh, green leaves on the cottonwoods are at their best in early summer.
DISTANCE:	3.7 miles one way
TRAIL RATING:	Easy to moderate, depending on how far you hike.
HIKING TIME:	1.5 to 3 hours
LOCATION:	4 miles from downtown Santa Fe
ELEVATION:	7,100 to 7,900 feet
SEASON:	Year-round access
MAPS:	Drake Mountain Maps: Mountains of Santa Fe; Santa Fe National Forest; USGS: Santa Fe
MANAGEMENT:	Santa Fe National Forest; private land
DIRECTIONS:	From downtown Santa Fe, travel north on Washington Avenue (NM 590) and drive 4 miles to County Road 72A. Make a right on CR 72A and travel 0.3 mile to the trailhead and parking.

creek. Go left and begin climbing away from the creek on this rocky path. After a short, steep ascent, you'll reach a junction with the Juan Trail on the right at the 1.1-mile mark. Bear left and continue climbing as the trail becomes quite narrow with steep drop-offs to the left down to Tesuque Creek.

You'll cross the creek for the second time at the 1.4-mile mark. This is the first of 14 creek crossings in the next 2 miles! The trail becomes wide as it passes through a beautiful, park-like ponderosa forest. Tall, old-growth ponderosa pines surround the trail, and the lovely Tesuque Creek flows freely on the left. This is a wonderful section of trail. Be on the lookout for early summer wildflowers along the banks of the creek and the moist, shaded areas.

The canyon narrows near the 2.0-mile mark and forces you to make several creek crossings. Rocks and logs help make these crossings easier, but it is still difficult to keep feet dry. At around the 2.6-mile mark, the trail becomes quite rough and makes two quick crossings of the creek. The canyon is very narrow through this section.

Cross the creek for the last time at the 3.2-mile mark, and climb up a short hill as the trail widens again and becomes smoother. The canyon opens into a lovely green meadow at the 3.7-mile mark. Tall willows line the creek, and wildflowers grow profusely in the sun-drenched meadow. You'll soon reach a junction with the Chamisa Trail and the turnaround point. The meadow is a lovely place to eat lunch and look for wildflowers before you retrace your steps back to the trailhead and your car.

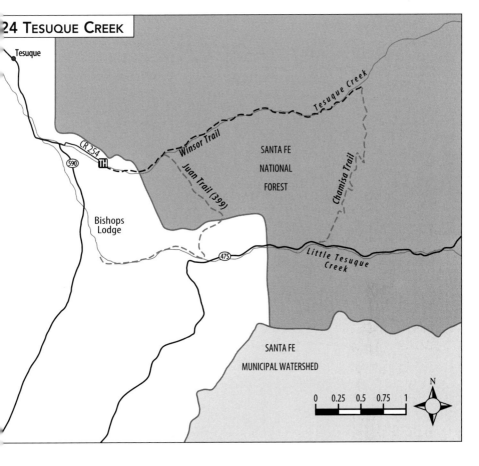

24 TESUQUE CREEK

Tesuque

CR 254

590

TH

Winsor Trail

Juan Trail (399)

SANTA FE

NATIONAL

FOREST

Tesuque Creek

Chamisa Trail

Bishops
Lodge

475

Little Tesuque
Creek

SANTA FE

MUNICIPAL WATERSHED

0   0.25   0.5   0.75   1

N

HIKE 25

DIABLO CANYON

As its name would suggest, this hike can be very hot in the summer, so be sure to bring plenty of water. Begin the hike by heading to the arroyo that leads into the canyon. Pass through a gate and beside a 300-foot basalt cliff on your right. Back in the early '70s, a group of climbers from Santa Fe (myself included) used these rocks for technical rock-climbing routes. The arroyo slices through the rocks and passes a small spring. On the other side of the rock wall, the arroyo widens and shoots toward Buckman Mesa before it veers left at the 1.6-mile mark and gently descends to the river.

The volcanic material in this area was left by the Caja del Rio volcanoes and the huge Jemez Caldera, 20 miles to the west. Pleasant hiking brings you to a road on the right; follow it to another road just before the lazy Rio Grande. Go left and you'll reach the Rio Grande and what used to be the Buckman Ranch. Enjoy the river before retracing the route back to your car.

MILEAGE/KEY POINTS

0.0 From the parking area, pass through a gate and hike toward the tall cliffs.

1.6 The arroyo veers left.

3.2 Arrive at the Rio Grande.

HIGHLIGHTS:	This year-round hike travels through a narrow canyon down to the Rio Grande.
DISTANCE:	3.2 miles one way
TRAIL RATING:	Easy, with very little elevation gain
HIKING TIME:	2 to 3 hours
LOCATION:	10 miles northwest of Santa Fe
ELEVATION:	5,900 to 5,480 feet
SEASON:	Year-round access
MAPS:	USGS: White Rock
MANAGEMENT:	Santa Fe National Forest
DIRECTIONS:	From the intersection of Paseo de Peralta and St. Francis Drive, travel north on US 84/285 (St. Francis Drive) to the exit for NM 599. Go west on NM 599 for 3.5 miles, turn right on Camino de la Tierra, and continue for 8.1 miles to a road on the left. Follow this road and park near a large, dry wash. The hike starts here.

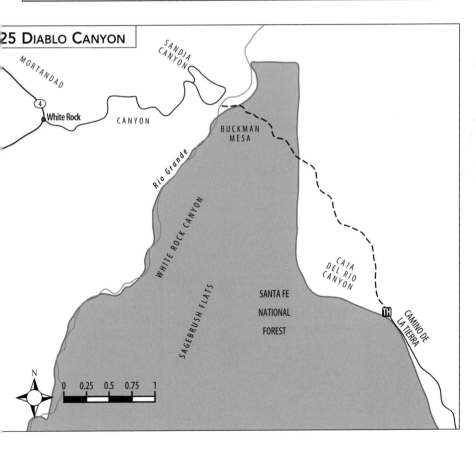

25 DIABLO CANYON

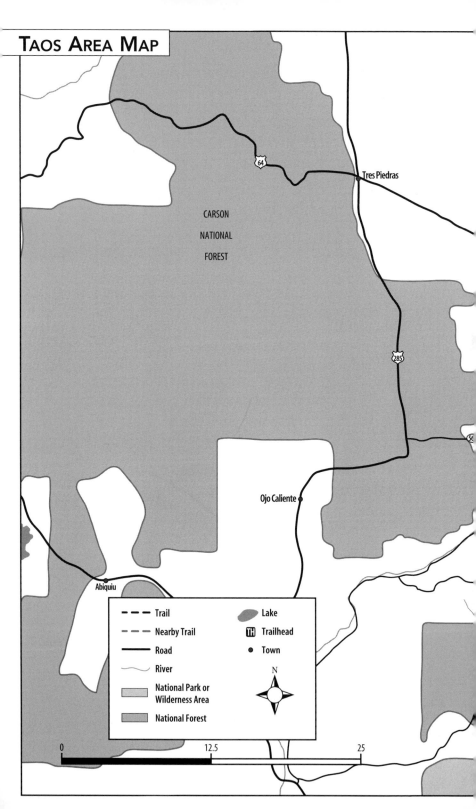

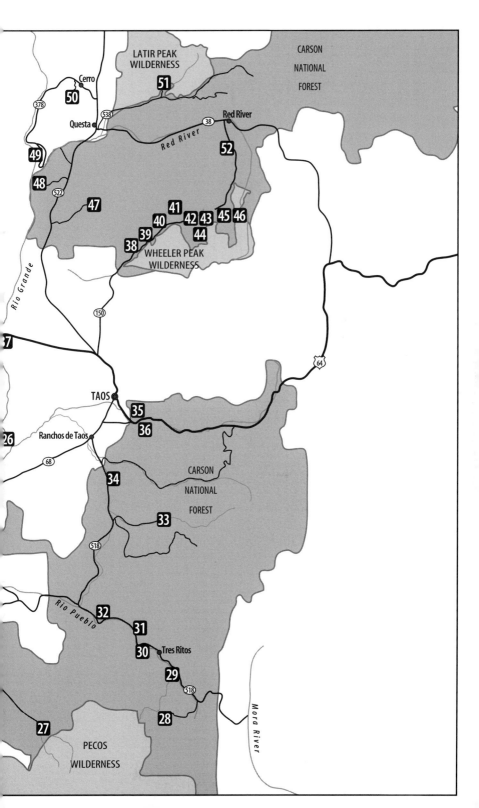

HIKE 26

LA VISTA VERDE TRAIL

Follow the trail from the parking area down some rocky steps and cross through a dry arroyo at the 0.4-mile mark. Numerous basalt (volcanic) rocks line the trail and the surrounding area.

MILEAGE/KEY POINTS
0.0 Trailhead and parking area.
0.6 A spur trail goes right and down to the river.
1.2 Arrive at a bench and great views.

Look carefully, and you may see remains of Native American pictographs and petroglyphs. Some of the larger rocks in the area have geometric designs believed to be 5,000 years old and human handprints that are 600 years old. Please look but don't touch, as oil from your fingers can fade and destroy this art.

An angler's trail at the 0.6-mile mark veers off to the right and down to the river. La Vista Verde Trail continues straight into a high-desert meadow filled with tall grass, cacti, and beautiful, old juniper and piñon trees. Pleasant hiking will soon bring you to a bench and the turnaround point for the hike.

Stop, sit, and enjoy the fantastic view up the Rio Grande Gorge and the sound of the Rio Grande. The fly-fishing in this section of the river is quite good, so bring a rod and some lunch, and make a day of it.

HIGHLIGHTS:	Solitude, scenic overlooks, fly-fishing, and beautiful desert trees highlight this short excursion along the Rio Grande.
DISTANCE:	1.2 miles one way
TRAIL RATING:	Easy, with very little elevation gain
HIKING TIME:	30 minutes to an hour
LOCATION:	20 miles south of Taos
ELEVATION:	7,300 to 7,400 feet
SEASON:	Year-round access
MAPS:	USGS: Taos County
MANAGEMENT:	BLM, Taos Resource Office
DIRECTIONS:	Travel south from Taos on NM 68 for 16 miles to Pilar. Turn right onto NM 570, and travel 6 miles along the lovely Rio Grande to the trailhead and parking on the right. The hike starts here.

26 LA VISTA VERDE TRAIL

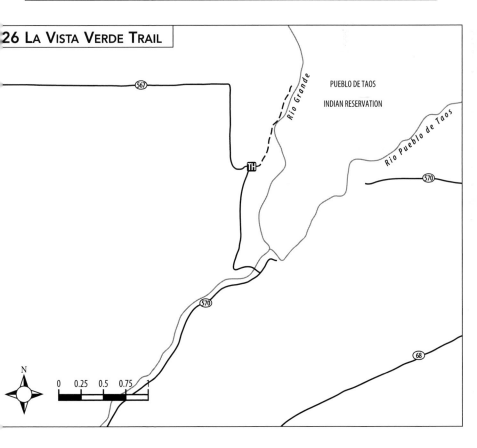

HIKE 27

TRAMPAS LAKES

HIGHLIGHTS:	One of the best hikes in the state, this trail up Trampas Canyon and along the beautiful Rio de las Trampas is resplendent with wildflowers and views and ends at a spectacular alpine cirque.
DISTANCE:	6.1 miles one way
TRAIL RATING:	Moderate to strenuous
HIKING TIME:	5 to 8 hours
LOCATION:	35 miles southwest of Taos
ELEVATION:	8,960 to 11,395 feet
SEASON:	June to late October
MAPS:	Carson National Forest; USGS: El Valle, Truchas Peaks
MANAGEMENT:	Carson National Forest/Pecos Wilderness
DIRECTIONS:	From the intersection of NM 518 and NM 68, travel south on NM 518 for 15.2 miles to NM 75. Go right and continue for 6.2 miles to NM 76. Go left and travel 4.4 miles to Forest Road 207, where you'll make another left and proceed 8.2 miles to the trailhead.

This is one of my favorite hikes in the state of New Mexico. A well-maintained trail, beautiful wildflowers, stunning alpine lakes, towering rock walls, and the lovely Rio de las Trampas contribute to the splendor of this trail. The area near the trailhead offers primitive camping and bathrooms. There is no running water, but the Rio de las Trampas can be used if it is treated.

MILEAGE/KEY POINTS

- **0.0** Trailhead and bathrooms. Go right on Trail 31.
- **0.7** Arrive at a small meadow.
- **1.0** Reach the Pecos Wilderness boundary.
- **2.3** Large scree slope.
- **2.5** Cross over the Rio de las Trampas.
- **2.6** Cross the stream again.
- **3.0** The first avalanche chute.
- **3.8** Switchbacks begin.
- **5.0** Cross the Rio de las Trampas.
- **6.0** Reach a trail junction.
- **6.1** Arrive at the lakes.

Start the hike by the bathrooms and access the marked Trail 31. The trail quickly climbs above the stream and reaches a lovely little meadow at the 0.7-mile mark. Young aspen trees thrive here, as do blooming wildflowers during the summer months. The trail climbs gently through a mixed-conifer forest and reaches a sign marking the Wilderness boundary at the 1.0-mile mark. Several spur trails lead down to some small waterfalls on the Rio de las Trampas.

Pleasant hiking through the dense forest leads past two large talus slopes. The second talus slope is particularly impressive, and the trail cuts right through the base of it. A short distance past the slope, you'll reach the Rio de las Trampas and cross it via a small log bridge. Wander up through an open meadow filled with skunk cabbage and wildflowers, and enjoy the open views down toward the trailhead. You'll cross the stream once more by way of a log bridge.

Impressive rock walls can be seen to the north, towering high above the trail. The hiking becomes level and quite pleasant through stands of tall pine and aspen. Wildflowers grow profusely here during the summer months, and the sound of the tumbling Rio de las Trampas is delightful music along this section of the hike. You'll soon pass by two large avalanche chutes. At the second chute the trail goes left, away from the stream, and climbs up through several long switchbacks. Stay on the trail (don't cut the switchbacks), and cross the stream once again at 5.0 miles. This makes for a great rest stop before tackling the last, steep mile of hiking to the lake.

The trail now climbs up at a steeper grade and crosses several small feeder streams that provide food for many water-loving flowers. This section of the trail stays wet and is rockier than the lower section of the trail. After a couple of short, steep switchbacks, you will arrive at a trail junction in a flat, marshy area. The trail to the right leads to Hidden Lake, Lower Trampas Lake is off to the left, and Upper Trampas Lake is straight ahead. The impressive Trampas Lakes are nestled below towering rock walls in a spectacular alpine cirque. The area around these lakes sees heavy foot traffic, so please camp in established sites and try not to tread on the fragile alpine vegetation.

This hike is particularly beautiful during the summer months of June, July, and early August. The wildflowers are at their peak, and the moist areas around the trail support a kaleidoscope of colorful beauties. Be on the lookout for Parry primrose, marsh marigold, thimbleberry, paintbrush, watercress, spiderwort, and various other wildflowers. I recommend Trampas Lake as an overnight destination, so you can fish, hike up one of the steep ridgelines or peaks near the lakes, and make the short (2 miles round trip) trek to Hidden Lake. As always, pack out all trash and dispose of human waste properly!

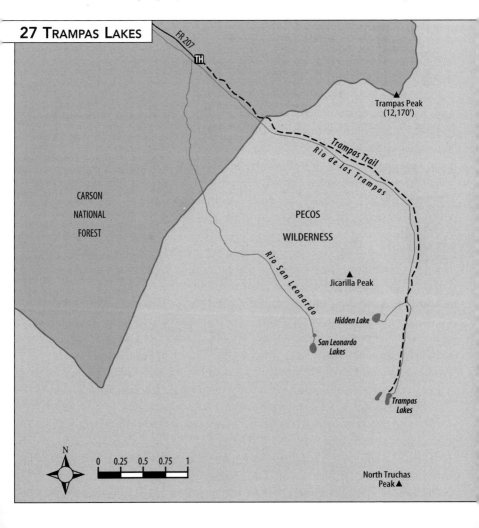

27 TRAMPAS LAKES

FR 207

TH

Trampas Peak
(12,170')

Trampas Trail

Rio de las Trampas

CARSON
NATIONAL
FOREST

PECOS

WILDERNESS

Rio San Leonardo

Jicarilla Peak

Hidden Lake

San Leonardo
Lakes

Trampas
Lakes

N

0   0.25   0.5   0.75   1

North Truchas
Peak ▲

HIKE 28

SERPENT LAKE

HIGHLIGHTS:	Serpent Lake, tucked beneath the towering summit of 12,835-foot Jicarita Peak, can be reached by this short and scenic trail flanked by early-season wildflowers.
DISTANCE:	3.3 miles one way
TRAIL RATING:	Moderate
HIKING TIME:	3 to 6 hours
LOCATION:	38 miles southeast of Taos
ELEVATION:	10,600 to 11,650 feet
SEASON:	Late May to late October
MAPS:	Carson National Forest; Trails Illustrated 730; USGS: Jicarita Peak, Holman.
MANAGEMENT:	Carson National Forest
DIRECTIONS:	From the intersection of NM 518 and NM 68, travel south on NM 518 for 29.5 miles to Forest Road 161. Turn right and continue 4.5 miles to the trailhead and small parking area.

From the parking area, continue straight on the road (Trail 19) and cross over several berms. (You will pass by the Angostura Trail, which goes right and down to NM 518.) Continue on the old four-wheel-drive road as it climbs up to another trail heading right into the woods at the 0.5-mile mark. (This is the Agua Piedra Trail,

MILEAGE/KEY POINTS

0.0 The Angostura Trail goes right; continue straight.

0.5 The Agua Piedra Trail goes right; continue straight and up on Trail 19.

0.7 Cross over Holman Ditch.

2.5 Reach the boundary of the Pecos Wilderness.

3.0 Reach a marked trail junction. Go right and down toward the lake.

3.3 Arrive at Serpent Lake.

which also goes right and drops down to NM 518.) Again, continue straight, and you will pass through a small, open meadow with a stream on the left. In early to mid-June, look along the stream for the delicate fairy slipper. This small orchid, also known as the calypso, thrives in the moist areas near the stream. I've seen several growing here.

At the 0.7-mile mark, you will arrive at the Holman Ditch. Go left across the ditch, and begin to climb on a narrow path through the pines. At 1.2 miles, the trail climbs up a series of steep switchbacks that wind through several small meadows filled with wildflowers in the early summer months. When you reach the 1.8-mile mark, the trail becomes quite rocky as it slices through an often-wet area filled with skunk cabbage and golden banner. You'll see a sign marking the boundary of the Pecos Wilderness at mile 2.5. The trail continues to climb and then makes a short descent to a trail marker. Views open to Jicarita Peak and its long, arching ridgeline.

Go right at the sign pointing the way to Serpent Lake. The trail drops quickly before entering a large, wet meadow. The lakes—there are more than one—sit in an impressive setting below the summit of Jicarita Peak. I find this to be one of the best early season wildflower hikes in the northern part of the state. On a trip here in late June, I saw chiming bells, alpine daisies, western red columbine, fairy slippers, marsh marigolds, and shooting stars, just to name a few. These lakes see little traffic, and there is not a defined trail going around them. Please use caution when exploring this fragile alpine environment.

This hike makes for a great two- or three-day backpack. There are several excellent campsites near Serpent Lake and in the trees near the trail junction, and you can set camp and spend time exploring the lakes or make the strenuous climb up to the summit of Jicarita Peak. The views from the peak are expansive and particularly impressive to the south, with the jagged summits of Truchas Peaks dominating the skyline.

28 SERPENT LAKE

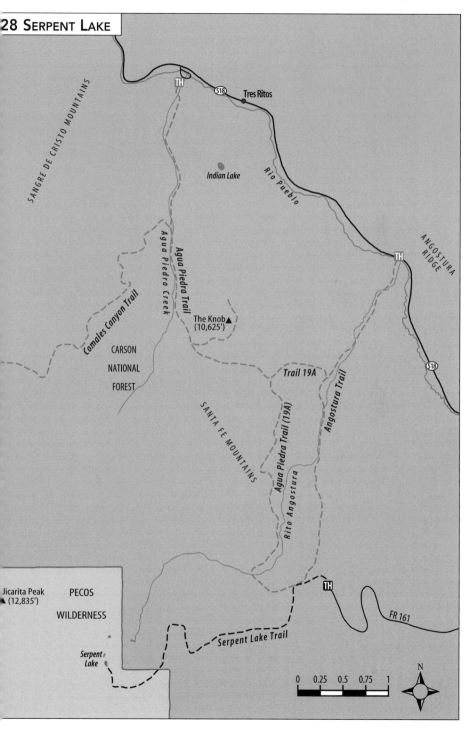

TH

518 **Tres Ritos**

SANGRE DE CRISTO MOUNTAINS

Indian Lake

Rio Pueblo

TH

ANGOSTURA RIDGE

Agua Piedra Creek

Agua Piedra Trail

Comales Canyon Trail

The Knob▲
(10,625')

CARSON

NATIONAL

FOREST

Trail 19A

Angostura Trail

SANTA FE MOUNTAINS

Agua Piedra Trail (19A)

Rito Angostura

518

Jicarita Peak
▲ (12,835')

PECOS

WILDERNESS

TH

FR 161

Serpent
Lake

Serpent Lake Trail

0   0.25   0.5   0.75   1

N

HIKE 29

ANGOSTURA TRAIL

HIGHLIGHTS:	Wildflowers, waterfalls, and solitude are yours on this seldom-hiked trail along the cascading Rito Angostura.
DISTANCE:	3.8 miles one way
TRAIL RATING:	Moderate
HIKING TIME:	3 to 6 hours
LOCATION:	38 miles southeast of Taos
ELEVATION:	10,600 to 11,650 feet
SEASON:	Late May to late October
MAPS:	Carson National Forest; Trails Illustrated 730; USGS: Holman, Jicarita Peak
MANAGEMENT:	Carson National Forest
DIRECTIONS:	From the intersection of NM 518 and NM 68, travel south on NM 518 for 27.6 miles to the unsigned trailhead on the right, across the Rio Pueblo.

Numerous trails shoot off from NM 518 along the Rio Pueblo. Most of them climb steeply to various peaks and Forest Service roads, often following small streams and narrow canyons over extremely rough terrain. The Angostura Trail is accompanied by the beautiful Rito Angostura as it winds up a narrow canyon through a beautiful, mixed forest to join the Alamitos Trail.

MILEAGE/KEY POINTS

0.0 From the trailhead, follow the rough double-track road up along the Rito Angostura.

0.8 Reach a trail marker.

1.0 Reach a junction with Agua Piedra Trail; continue straight.

1.5 Reach an unmarked trail junction; continue straight.

2.3 Arrive at the waterfall.

3.8 Reach the junction with Alamitos Trail and the turnaround point.

This hike starts at an unmarked trailhead just off NM 518 and follows a rough double-track road past some beautiful flower-filled meadows. You'll pass several summer homes before coming to a trail marker. Continue straight past the marker, and proceed over two berms and a stream crossing to a trail junction. (The Agua Piedra Trail heads off to the right.) You'll begin a gradual climb up to another trail junction, at the 1.5-mile mark. Continue straight on the wide singletrack trail into a grove of tall pines and aspens beside the Rito Angostura. The already beautiful hiking along this section is highlighted by multi-colored wildflowers that cover the steep hillsides during the summer months.

At around the 1.8-mile mark, you'll reach the crest of a hill and trot down to a small stream crossing. A gentle climb leads to a pleasant surprise at the 2.3-mile mark. The lovely little waterfall on the right marks a great place to stop for a short break. I always enjoy the sounds of the woods and the soothing water in this beautiful spot.

Beyond the waterfall the trail cuts through a small, open meadow filled with wildflowers and begins to gain altitude quickly. The route becomes very rocky at the 3.3-mile mark and then levels out for a short distance before tackling a very short (and very steep) hill. At the top of the hill, the trail meets with the Alamitos Trail and the turnaround point. Retrace the route back to the trailhead and your car.

29 ANGOSTURA TRAIL

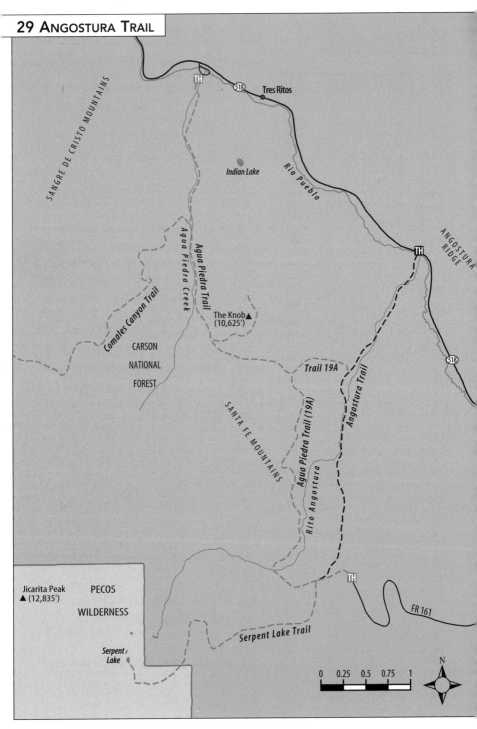

SANGRE DE CRISTO MOUNTAINS

TH

518 Tres Ritos

Indian Lake

Rio Pueblo

ANGOSTURA RIDGE

TH

Agua Piedra Creek

Agua Piedra Trail

Comales Canyon Trail

The Knob ▲
(10,625')

CARSON

NATIONAL

FOREST

Trail 19A

SANTA FE MOUNTAINS

Angostura Trail

518

Agua Piedra Trail (19A)

Rito Angostura

Jicarita Peak
▲ (12,835')

PECOS

WILDERNESS

TH

FR 161

Serpent Lake Trail

Serpent
Lake

0   0.25   0.5   0.75   1

N

HIKE 30

AGUA PIEDRA TRAIL

This is a nice hike up through several open meadows to the rounded summit of The Knob. The trail is popular and can get crowded during the summer months. Hikers, mountain bikers, ATVs, and equestrians use this trail for enjoyment and to access the many different trails in the area. Please show respect to other users and remember that each group has a right to enjoy these public lands.

Follow the wide trail into the pine trees. A large meadow will be on your right. Climb at a gentle rate, and you'll soon reach a trail on the left that leads up to Indian Lake. Continue straight and pass through a gate at the 0.5-mile mark. The trail becomes very wide and rocky before crossing over Agua Piedra Creek. It then climbs into a meadow filled with tall, green grasses and wildflowers during the summer months. The trail winds through the tall pines and then crosses the creek two more times before it reaches a junction with the Comales Canyon Trail (sign reads Ripley's Point Trail) on the right at the 1.5-mile mark. (This trail climbs up to Ripley's Point and the Skyline Trail that leads to Jicarita Peak, to the south.) Continue straight, climbing through a nice meadow and then back into the trees on the west side of the creek.

The trail steepens, and you'll soon arrive at an open area and fence line at the 2.5-mile mark. (A faint trail goes left along the fence and leads to

MILEAGE/KEY POINTS

0.0	Start at the sign marking the trail and pass through a gate.
0.3	Junction with the Indian Lake Trail; continue straight.
0.5	Pass through a gate.
1.3	Cross Agua Piedra Creek.
1.5	Junction with Comales Canyon Trail; continue straight.
2.5	Reach an open area and fence line.
3.5	Junction with Trail 19A and the turnaround point.

HIGHLIGHTS:	Agua Piedra Trail passes through several open, wildflower-filled meadows as it winds along beautiful Agua Piedra Creek.
DISTANCE:	3.5 miles one way
TRAIL RATING:	Moderate (with a steady climb up to The Knob, if desired)
HIKING TIME:	2 to 3.5 hours
LOCATION:	28 miles southeast of Taos
ELEVATION:	8,400 to 10,000 feet
SEASON:	Early spring to late fall
MAPS:	Trails Illustrated 730; Carson National Forest; USGS: Jicarita Peak, Tres Ritos
MANAGEMENT:	Carson National Forest
DIRECTIONS:	From the junction of NM 518 and NM 75, travel east on NM 518 for 7 miles to the Agua Piedra Campground on the right. Turn right into the campground, cross over the Rio Pueblo, and turn left. Follow the road till it terminates at a holding pen and the trailhead. The hike starts here.

the summit of The Knob.) Continue on the main trail and through several open areas before dropping down into a meadow and a junction with Trail 19A and the turnaround point. Views open to the Jicarita Peak ridgeline, and this pleasant spot makes for a wonderful place to take a break and enjoy some food in the beautiful surroundings. After your time in the meadow, retrace your route back to the trailhead and your car.

You can easily extend your hiking time and mileage by connecting with one of the many trails that are in the area. Bring a map and explore to your heart's content. I also bring my fly rod when I am in the area, so I can spend some time fishing the lovely Rio Pueblo. This catch-and-release stream is home to native cutthroat trout.

0 AGUA PIEDRA TRAIL

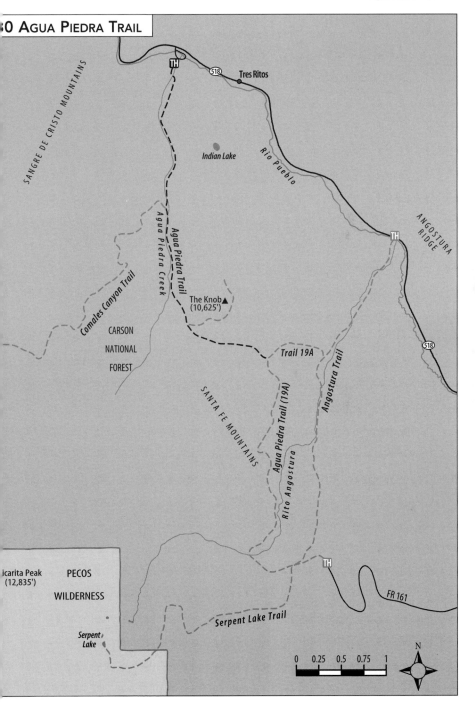

TH
518 Tres Ritos

SANGRE DE CRISTO MOUNTAINS

Indian Lake

Rio Pueblo

ANGOSTURA RIDGE

TH

Agua Piedra Creek

Agua Piedra Trail

Comales Canyon Trail

The Knob ▲
(10,625')

Trail 19A

518

CARSON

NATIONAL

FOREST

SANTA FE MOUNTAINS

Agua Piedra Trail (19A)

Angostura Trail

Rito Angostura

icarita Peak
(12,835')

PECOS

WILDERNESS

TH

FR 161

Serpent Lake Trail

Serpent
Lake

0   0.25   0.5   0.75   1

N

FLECHADO CANYON TRAIL TO GALLEGOS PEAK

Photo by William Stone

From the campground, cross the highway and look west for a trail marker. The trail weaves into Flechado Canyon and begins a steep climb along the creek. Lush vegetation thrives here during the summer months. After a mile of climbing in the narrow canyon, the trail enters a lovely meadow filled with stately aspen trees and colorful wildflowers.

Beyond the meadow, the trail crosses the stream several times and climbs steeply on rocky tread into a mixed-conifer forest. Here the trail stays steep and soon reaches a junction with the Gallegos Peak Trail, an old logging road. Gallegos Peak lies to the east and is a short jaunt on this road.

When the road divides, you'll take the right fork. The road soon narrows to a path before reaching a trail junction at a signless post. Go left and climb steeply to the summit of Gallegos Peak. Expansive views south to Jicarita Peak and the triple summits of the Truchas Peaks make the extra effort to reach the top of Gallegos worthwhile.

MILEAGE/KEY POINTS	
0.0	Cross the highway and access the start of the trail.
1.0	Enter a lovely, aspen-filled meadow.
1.7	The trail becomes steep and rocky.
2.4	Arrive at a junction with the Gallegos Peak Trail.
2.7	Road divides; take the right fork.
2.9	Arrive at a junction with signless post; turn left.
3.0	The summit of Gallegos Peak.

HIGHLIGHTS:	The seldom-traveled trail to Gallegos Peak is short, steep, and beautiful. A lovely mountain stream accompanies you through rugged Flechado Canyon and into a meadow filled with wildflowers and flanked by aspens.
DISTANCE:	3 miles one way
TRAIL RATING:	Moderate, with a steep climb in the first mile
HIKING TIME:	2.5 to 4.5 hours
LOCATION:	25 miles southeast of Taos
ELEVATION:	8,000 to 10,528 feet
SEASON:	Early spring to late fall
MAPS:	Carson National Forest; Trails Illustrated 730; USGS: Tres Ritos
MANAGEMENT:	Carson National Forest
DIRECTIONS:	From the junction of NM 518 and NM 75, travel east on NM 518 for 5.4 miles to the Flechado Canyon Campground on the right. The hike starts across the highway.

31 FLECHADO CANYON TRAIL TO GALLEGOS PEAK

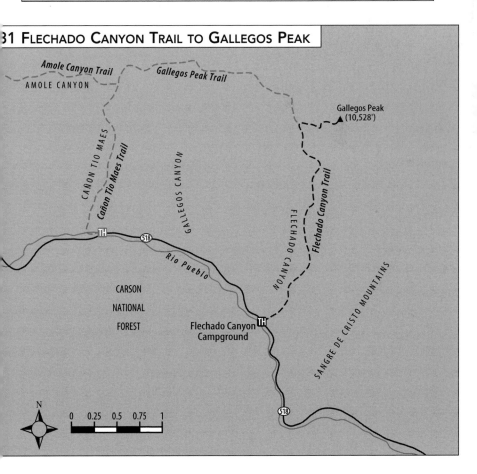

HIKE 32

CAÑON TIO MAES

HIGHLIGHTS:	"Short and sweet" best describes this beautiful hike through rugged, rocky Cañon Tio Maes, and a flower-filled meadow is your reward.
DISTANCE:	2 miles one way
TRAIL RATING:	Moderate, with a steep climb in the first mile
HIKING TIME:	1.5 to 3 hours
LOCATION:	25 miles southeast of Taos
ELEVATION:	8,000 to 9,200 feet
SEASON:	Early spring to late fall
MAPS:	Trails Illustrated 730; Carson National Forest; USGS: Tres Ritos
MANAGEMENT:	Carson National Forest
DIRECTIONS:	From the junction of NM 518 and NM 75, travel east on NM 518 for 3.1 miles to a turnoff on the left. Go left over the Rio Pueblo, and make a quick right into a small parking area and the trailhead.

From the parking area, climb up past the sign and through a gate into Cañon Tio Maes. The trail climbs steeply along a stream on the west side of the canyon. The trail is very rocky and gains elevation quickly through the narrow and rugged

MILEAGE/KEY POINTS
0.0 Start at the trail sign and pass through a gate.
1.0 Enter a lovely, aspen-filled meadow.
2.0 Arrive at a junction with the Amole Canyon Trail and the turn-around point.

canyon. After a mile of steep hiking, you'll enter a lovely, aspen-filled meadow replete with wildflowers during the summer months.

The trail continues to climb, now at a gentle grade, through stands of aspen and into a large clearing, passing several old logging roads. The route veers right and soon reaches a junction with the Amole Canyon Trail and the turnaround point.

You can extend your hike by going right on the Amole Canyon Trail to reach the Gallegos Peak Trail, which takes you an additional 3 miles to Gallegos Peak. From any of these points, simply retrace your route back to the trailhead to complete the hike.

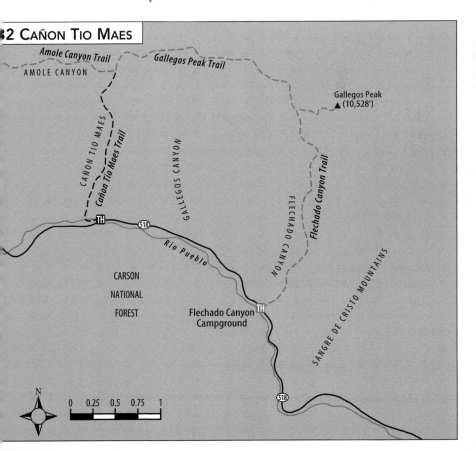

32 CAÑON TIO MAES

BERNARDIN LAKE

Photo by Mike Butterfield

HIGHLIGHTS:	Gorgeous, flower-filled meadows and a lovely lake are the gems of this seldom-done hike along the picturesque Rito de la Olla.
DISTANCE:	5 miles one way
TRAIL RATING:	Moderate, with a steep climb to the lake
HIKING TIME:	2.5 to 4.5 hours
LOCATION:	15 miles southeast of Taos
ELEVATION:	8,600 to 9,450 feet
SEASON:	Late spring to late fall
MAPS:	Carson National Forest; Trails Illustrated 730; USGS: Shadybrook
MANAGEMENT:	Carson National Forest
DIRECTIONS:	Drive 7 miles south on NM 518 to Forest Road 438, just past Pot Creek. Turn left on FR 438 and follow it for 6 miles to the trailhead at a metal gate. The hike starts here.

Start the hike by passing through the metal gate. The narrow trail used to be a Forest Service road. Now that it is closed to vehicles, the road is being reclaimed by nature. The first section of the hike goes up through a narrow canyon, reaches a rockslide area, and then crosses the lovely Rito de la Olla on a wooden bridge. The trail climbs up a short hill and then crosses the stream again, this time near a dilapidated bridge at roughly 1 mile.

After the second stream crossing, the trail becomes very quaint as it cuts through several stands of tall willows. Look for

MILEAGE/KEY POINTS	
0.0	Start by passing through the gate.
0.4	Rockslide area.
0.7	Cross over a small wooden bridge.
0.8	Cross a stream at a dilapidated bridge.
1.7	Pass through a stand of tall willows.
2.1	Reach an open meadow that is filled with wildflowers during the summer months.
2.6	Reach a trail junction; continue straight.
3.8	Beautiful tarns and beaver ponds on the right.
4.3	Reach the first of the berms.
4.4	Go left at the fifth berm and up an old, double-track road.
4.8	Go right at the top of the ridge.
5.0	Reach Bernardin Lake and the turnaround point.

beaver activity near the trail and to the right along the stream. As you continue along this mellow trail, you'll pass through the first of several meadows—a wildflower-lover's paradise during the months of June, July, and August. This is a good spot to take a break and enjoy the tranquility.

The trail comes to a road junction at the 2.6-mile mark. The road heads right, over the stream, and you continue straight on the nice trail up to another flower-filled meadow. You'll reach a nice little spot with several tarns on the right at the 3.8-mile mark. Look around at the willows and notice the clean cutting done by beavers. Tall meadow grasses surround the tarns and water-loving wildflowers grow along the banks. This is quite a picturesque little spot!

Continue heading straight to reach the first of several berms, designed to prevent vehicles from using the trail. Begin counting, for at the fifth berm you'll go left and follow a rocky double-track road up into an open meadow. The trail narrows and climbs up through this grassy expanse, veering to the right and climbing up to a ridge. Go right at the top of the ridge, then follow the road through a nice conifer forest. The trail levels and then makes a short drop down to the lake, which is nestled on a small shelf. The last time I was here, Bernardin Lake was nearly dry due to lack of rain and snowfall. Hopefully, when you do the hike, the lake will be full and glistening again. The hillsides here are typically covered with wildflowers, and the lake makes for a great spot to eat lunch, relax, and enjoy the solitude before you retrace your route back to the trailhead and your car.

I have hiked this trail several times and have rarely encountered another person. The open meadows, the wildflowers, the lovely stream, and the beauty of the surrounding hills makes me wonder why this trail doesn't see more foot traffic. It is a well-kept secret!

33 BERNARDIN LAKE

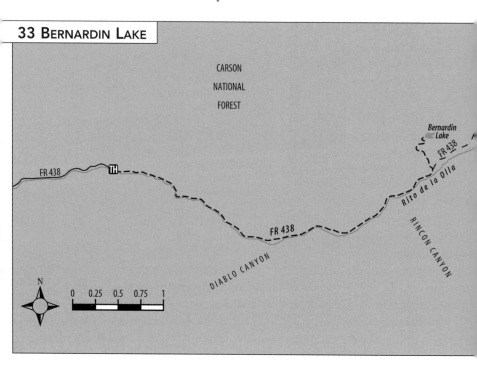

HIKE 34

RIO GRANDE DEL RANCHO TRAIL

Don't let the mileage scare you away from this hike. The easy-to-access trail is close to town and offers a wonderful trek into the beautiful foothills below Tetillas Peak. You can make your adventure as short or as long as your time and energy allow!

Start the hike by crossing NM 518 to the start of the trail, which is on the east side of the highway. Follow the narrow and rocky path up a short hill to a junction with a wide, double-track trail. Go right, following the pleasant trail through the trees. At the 0.9-mile mark the road/trail veers to the right across a drainage—the first of several in the next few miles. Notice the green grass, cottonwood trees, wildflowers, and willows that thrive in these moist areas surrounded by high desert.

The trail continues to head south, accompanied by great views. Cross through several

MILEAGE/KEY POINTS
0.0 Cross (with caution) NM 518 to access the trail, on the north side of the road.
0.2 Go right at the top of the hill.
0.9 The road veers right across a drainage.
1.6 Another drainage.
2.2 Another drainage.
3.1 A road goes left up to Tetillas Peak; continue on the trail.
3.3 Reach a junction; continue straight.
5.6 Arrive at a nice, open meadow.
5.7 Arrive at the junction with FR 438 and Rito de la Olla, the turnaround point.

HIGHLIGHTS:	Its proximity to town and almost year-round access make this hike through the beautiful piñon- and juniper-covered hills near Taos a good outing for the whole family.
DISTANCE:	5.7 miles one way
TRAIL RATING:	Easy, with very little elevation change
HIKING TIME:	2.5 to 4.5 hours
LOCATION:	3 miles southeast of Taos
ELEVATION:	7,200 to 7,550 feet
SEASON:	Year-round access
MAPS:	Carson National Forest; Trails Illustrated 730
MANAGEMENT:	Carson National Forest
DIRECTIONS:	From Taos, go south on NM 68 to NM 518 and turn left. Travel 2.8 miles on NM 578 to the trailhead parking area on the right at a guardrail. The hike starts here.

more moist areas, and drop down a hill and then up to a junction with a road on the left at 3.1 miles. (This road climbs steeply up to Tetillas Peak.) Hikers who are short on time might want to turn around here and return to the trailhead.

Continue heading straight, and you'll soon arrive at another trail junction at 3.3 miles. Head straight here, as well. The trail now becomes wide and the views open to the east, south, and north. Several spur roads shoot off to the right and down to NM 518. The Pot Creek Cultural Site, which includes several Anasazi dwellings occupied around 1200 AD, lies to the south near NM 518. The center is open from late May to early September and offers several interesting programs and tours. Make it a point to stop at this fine site to learn about the early times and lives of the local Tewa-speaking people.

Near the 5.3-mile mark, you'll be able to see some of the cultural sites on the right. There are several crisscrossing routes here; just keep heading straight. You'll soon arrive at a beautiful meadow at the 5.6-mile mark. At 5.7 miles, you'll reach a junction with Forest Road 438 and the Rito de la Olla—the turnaround point.

34 RIO GRANDE DEL RANCHO TRAIL

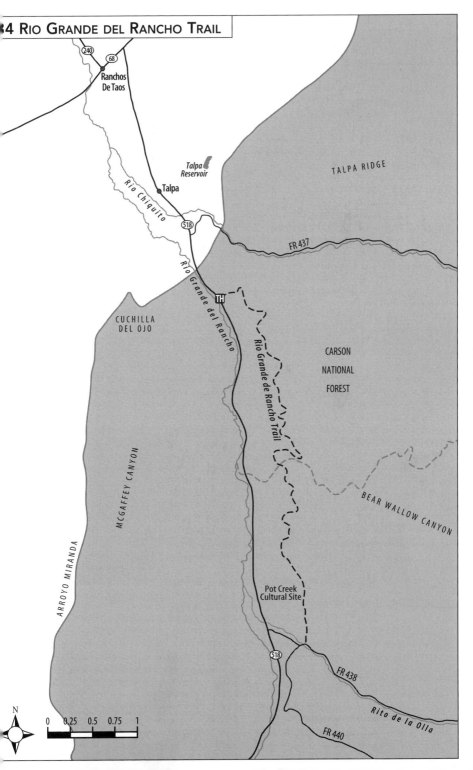

The foothills surrounding the Taos area are populated by piñon and juniper trees. A mature piñon takes roughly 250 years to reach a height of 25 to 30 feet. A mature juniper tree takes twice as long—up to 500 years—to reach the same height. These beautiful trees are symbols of the high desert environment and should be treated with great respect. Cutting them destroys centuries of growth, and irrevocably changes the landscape.

Piñon trees are at great risk in this area due to a beetle infestation that, with the help of the recent drought, has killed hundreds of thousands of pines in northern New Mexico. When pine bark beetles attack a healthy tree, the sap drowns or pushes them out of the trunk, protecting the tree from permanent damage. However, the trees become weak during times of drought and are unable to produce sap. Beetles can feed on the drought-ridden trees unopposed, and the insects are reproducing—and devouring—at a rapid rate.

Things don't look good for the piñon, New Mexico's state tree. Unless the area receives more moisture, we will lose an integral part of the landscape and culture of the Land of Enchantment.

Piñon trees and Penitente Cross.

HIKE 35

DEVISADARO PEAK LOOP

HIGHLIGHTS:	This local favorite is close to town and has almost year-round access. Beautiful hiking through piñon and juniper trees and great views from Devisadaro's summit make the loop particularly special.
DISTANCE:	6 mile loop
TRAIL RATING:	Moderate, with a steep, rocky climb to Devisadaro Peak
HIKING TIME:	1.5 to 2.5 hours
LOCATION:	2 miles southeast of Taos
ELEVATION:	7,200 to 8,304 feet
SEASON:	Early spring to late fall
MAPS:	Carson National Forest; Trails Illustrated 730; USGS: Palo Flechado Pass
MANAGEMENT:	Carson National Forest
DIRECTIONS:	From the junction of US 64 and NM 68, travel east on US 64 for 2.8 miles to the trailhead on the left. (The El Nogal Picnic Area will be on your right.)

The trail, which starts directly off US 64, climbs up through piñon and juniper trees, passing under some power lines before turning to the east. You'll reach a signed trail junction for Devisadaro Trail 108 at the 0.5-mile mark. This is where the loop section of the hike begins. Go right (the easier option), and continue climbing through the trees. You'll enjoy several level stretches of trail before a steep and rocky section brings you to the top of Devisadaro Peak at roughly 2.5 miles.

MILEAGE/KEY POINTS

0.0 Follow the well-marked Devisadaro Trail uphill.

0.5 Reach a signed trail junction and the start of the loop; go right.

2.5 Reach the top of Devisadaro Peak and the chairs.

3.0 Arrive at a junction with the North Boundary Trail on the right; continue left on the Devisadaro Trail.

5.5 Reach the end of the loop-portion of the hike.

6.0 Arrive at your car and the trailhead.

Take advantage of the stone seats that have been constructed by hikers, and enjoy the great views east up Taos Canyon and Valle Escondido. Just beyond the chairs is a USGS marker for Devisadaro Peak. From here, you have two options: Retrace your route back to the trailhead, or continue straight to finish the loop. As variety is the spice of life, I recommend doing the entire loop.

The trail starts to drop steeply on the east side of the mountain and soon reaches a junction with the North Boundary Trail. (The North Boundary Trail follows a ridgeline and eventually meets with the Capulin Trail in lovely Capulin Canyon.) Go left at the trail junction, and enjoy wonderful hiking through mixed spruce and fir on the north side of the mountain. The trail turns south and traverses along the south side of the mountain, crossing several small canyons and seasonal drainages. Views open to Taos and the plains west to the Rio Grande Gorge. The trail then climbs to reach the end of the loop at the marked sign. Drop steeply back to the trailhead and your car.

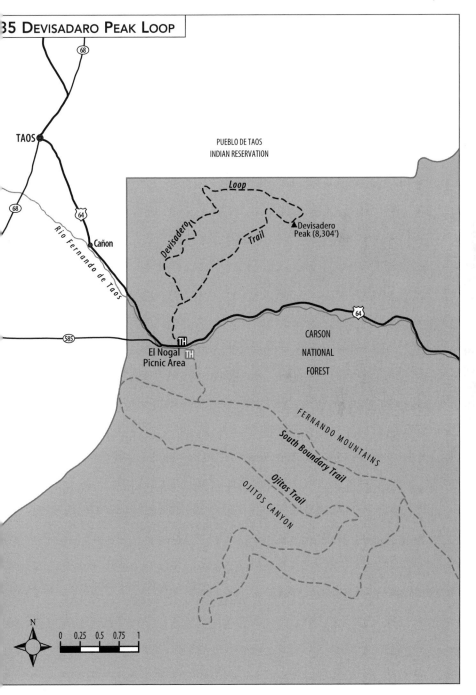

35 DEVISADARO PEAK LOOP

68

TAOS

68

64

Rio Fernando de Taos

Cañon

585

El Nogal
Picnic Area

TH
TH

PUEBLO DE TAOS
INDIAN RESERVATION

Loop

Devisadero

Trail

▲ Devisadero
Peak (8,304')

64

CARSON

NATIONAL

FOREST

FERNANDO MOUNTAINS

South Boundary Trail

Ojitos Trail

OJITOS CANYON

N

0   0.25   0.5   0.75   1

HIKE 36

SOUTH BOUNDARY TRAIL

Start the hike by crossing a bridge over the Rio Fernando. Go right on the South Boundary Trail, climbing through a series of switchbacks along a fence line. At the 0.3-mile mark, the trail meets the fence and veers to the left (east). The trail climbs through piñon and juniper up to more switchbacks at the 1.0-mile mark.

The hiking becomes steep and rocky as the trail reaches the crest of a small ridge with good views north to Taos Mountain and south to Ojitos Canyon. Here the grade eases, and the hiking becomes quite pleasant. Wildflowers and cacti bloom on the sunny hillside during May and June, adding color to the brown, high-desert environment. Look for the sweet-smelling mock orange flower and western wallflower.

At around the 2 mile mark, the trail begins to climb in earnest. The trees start to thin, and the vegetation changes from piñon and juniper to ponderosa pine, the predominant tree of the Transition Zone. The trail hugs the side of the ridge as views of Wheeler Peak and Taos Mountain fill the eastern skyline. It's difficult to believe you are a mere stone's throw from downtown Taos!

Around the 3-mile mark, the trail enters a mixed-conifer forest and becomes quite narrow and rocky. As you head due east, you'll see views open up to Taos Canyon, Valle Escondido, and Sierra de Don Fernando Peak. The trail veers to the south through a small aspen

MILEAGE/KEY POINTS	
0.0	Begin at the marked South Boundary Trail 164, across the bridge from the El Nogal Picnic Area.
0.3	Go left at the fence line.
1.0	Go right at a tight switchback.
3.8	Arrive at a junction with Ojitos Canyon Trail and the turnaround point.

HIGHLIGHTS:	This convenient and scenic hike provides a taste of the 22-mile-long South Boundary Trail.
DISTANCE:	3.8 miles one way
TRAIL RATING:	Moderate, with a steady climb up to the turnaround point
HIKING TIME:	1.5 to 2.5 hours
LOCATION:	2 miles southeast of Taos
ELEVATION:	7,200 to 9,200 feet
SEASON:	Early spring to late fall
MAPS:	Trails Illustrated 730; Carson National Forest; USGS: Palo Flechado Pass
MANAGEMENT:	Carson National Forest
DIRECTIONS:	From the junction of US 64 and NM 68, travel east on US 64 for 2.8 miles to the trailhead and parking at the El Nogal Picnic Area.

forest and reaches a junction with the Ojitos Canyon Trail and the turnaround point.

The Ojitos Canyon Trail shoots off to the right and heads down Ojitos Canyon back to NM 68—a fun route to try if you have the time. The South Boundary Trail continues to climb for a short distance and then takes a level line across Fernando Mountain. It passes through a beautiful forest of pine and aspen into Garcia Park and over Quintana Pass before dropping down to the small village of Black Lake. The 22-mile route was once the dividing line between two large land grants, the Taos and Rio Grande del Rancho, giving the trail its name. Feel free to keep exploring if time and your endurance allow!

36 SOUTH BOUNDARY TRAIL

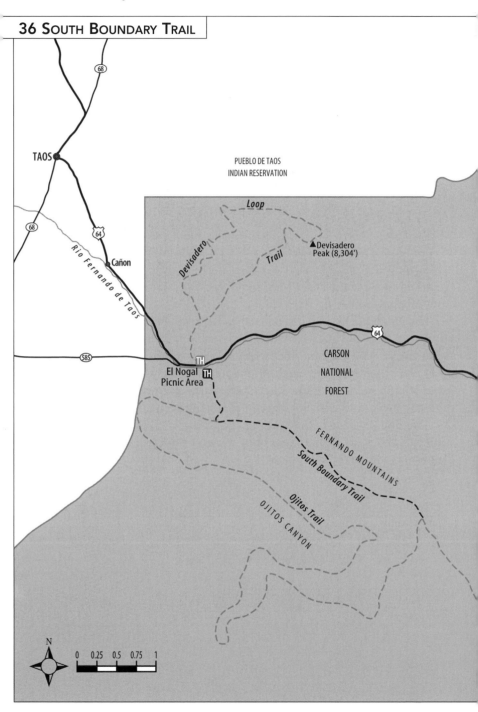

Hike 37

WEST RIM TRAIL

HIGHLIGHTS:	Views, solitude, the spectacular Rio Grande Gorge, and the river itself highlight this year-round hike close to Taos.
DISTANCE:	8.7 miles one way.
TRAIL RATING:	Easy to moderate, depending on distance
HIKING TIME:	1 to 6 hours
LOCATION:	10 miles northwest of Taos
ELEVATION:	6,500 to 6,700 feet
SEASON:	Year-round access
MAPS:	USGS: Taos County
MANAGEMENT:	BLM, Taos Field Office
DIRECTIONS:	From the intersection of NM 150 and US 64 just north of Taos, follow US 64 west for 6.7 miles to a rest area and trailhead on the west side of the Rio Grande Gorge Bridge. The hike starts near a fence line on the south side of the rest area.

This is a far-as-you-like-to-go hike, as the total out-and-back is 17.4 miles. My recommendation would be to hike at a leisurely pace and stop at one of the many overlooks along the trail. The trail hugs the edge of the spectacular Rio Grande Gorge on a sage-covered

MILEAGE/KEY POINTS

0.0 Fence line and trailhead.
2.7 Trail junction.
4.2 Trail junction.
5.2 Overlook.
6.3 Overlook and power lines; veer right
8.7 Trailhead at NM 567 and turn-around point.

mesa with beautiful views in all directions. Fall, winter, and early spring are the best times to do the hike, as summer heat can be quite staggering on the open mesa. Bring lots of water, as you'll be hiking through high-desert country, and there is little shade for relief from the sun.

Start the hike by passing through the gate. The dramatic Rio Grande Gorge Bridge lies just north and stretches a quarter of a mile across the river, connecting US 64 with the east and west sides of the river. The trail drops a bit in elevation and angles left toward the rim of the gorge. Several benches along the trail make for pleasant stopping points from which to enjoy the spectacular scenery. The trail is marked well with BLM signposts and is quite easy to follow. This mesa is classic high-desert country, home to rattlesnakes, red ants, coyotes, jackrabbits, raptors, and, occasionally, humans in their earth-ship homes.

Around the 2.7-mile mark, there is a wonderful overlook on the left with great views into the deep gorge. Several basalt cliffs line the gorge—telltale signs of the volcanic activity in the area's past. Contrary to some beliefs, the Rio Grande did not carve its way through the gorge. This section of the river flows through an area known as the Rio Grande Rift Valley. The earth's crust literally dropped between opposing faults, leaving a huge channel—a perfect riverbed.

Continue straight past the overlook, enjoying expansive views in all directions. Taos Mountain and high summits of the Wheeler Peak Wilderness dominate the eastern skyline. An endless sea of sage and sky flow west to the obvious landmark of Tres Piedras (three rocks). To the north, the impressive Gorge Bridge arches over the Rio Grande, and one can see a hundred miles to Colorado and the 14,000-foot summits of Little Bear and Blanca Peaks beyond. The Rio Grande continues its journey south through the state of New Mexico, giving much needed water to a very arid land.

You'll reach a junction at 4.2 miles. The many roads that crisscross the mesa were once used for harvesting wood and piñon nuts. Beware of the red-ant mounds that line the trail along this section of the hike: Red ants bite! (Unfortunately, I speak from experience.)

At the 5.2-mile mark, you'll reach another overlook, with great views down to the river. You'll then pass some power lines and veer right, entering the sage country. Several earth-ship homes lie off to the west, adding interesting flavor to the area. After 2.5 more miles of hiking, you will reach the trailhead at NM 567 and the turnaround point of the hike. Feel free to hike as far as time and your endurance will allow, but remember that you'll have to hike back, and there is very little relief from the sun out here. Bring a load of water and some energy bars for a hearty snack.

Note: I find this hike to be more enjoyable when I set a shuttle at both ends of the trail. This way, I can hike the whole distance without worrying about the time, and I avoid retracing the route.

Beautiful and sacred Taos Mountain.

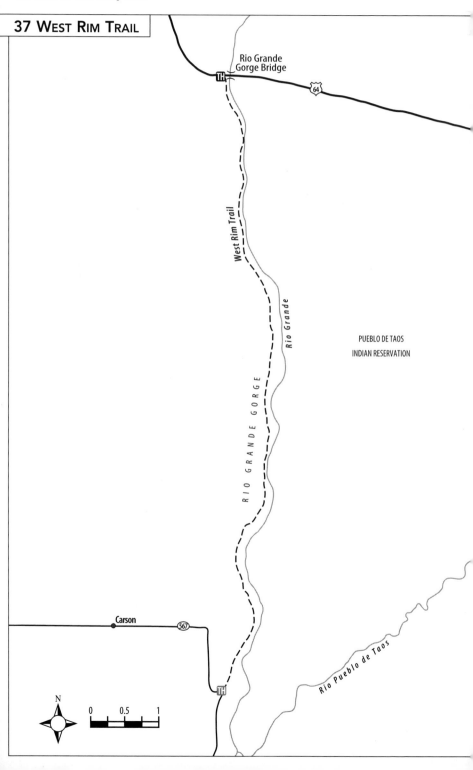

37 WEST RIM TRAIL

Rio Grande
Gorge Bridge

TH

64

West Rim Trail

Rio Grande

RIO GRANDE GORGE

PUEBLO DE TAOS
INDIAN RESERVATION

Carson

567

TH

Rio Pueblo de Taos

N

0   0.5   1

HIKE 38

YERBA CANYON

HIGHLIGHTS:	If you crave a challenge and some stellar scenery, this steep and difficult day hike up through beautiful Yerba Canyon is a great choice!
DISTANCE:	4.2 miles one way
TRAIL RATING:	Strenuous, with an elevation gain of 3,200 feet in less than 4 miles
HIKING TIME:	4 to 7 hours
LOCATION:	15 miles northeast of Taos
ELEVATION:	8,400 to 11,600 feet
SEASON:	Late June to late October
MAPS:	Carson National Forest; USGS: Arroyo Seco, Wheeler Peak
MANAGEMENT:	Carson National Forest
DIRECTIONS:	From Taos, travel north on US 64 to NM 150. Turn right and travel 10.1 miles to the trailhead on the left. Park along the road or go left up a short, steep hill to a small parking area at the trailhead proper.

The trail up Yerba Canyon is steep and difficult. It follows a narrow path up a steep canyon along a beautiful mountain stream flanked by lush vegetation during the summer months. This route is best for experienced hikers in good physical condition.

Follow the trail into a narrow canyon, crossing the creek several times within the first mile. The trail stays close to this little stream, and wildflowers grow profusely in the moist, fertile soil. Wild geranium, paintbrush, baneberry, willow, and other water-loving plants can be found along this section of the trail. In fact, wildflower lovers could spend most of their time on this stretch of the trail, simply identifying flowers.

MILEAGE/KEY POINTS

0.0 Trailhead and bathroom.
0.5 Arrive at the first of several stream crossings.
1.0 Stream crossing at a small waterfall.
1.4 Another stream crossing.
1.8 Begin a series of long, steep switchbacks.
3.0 Small, beautiful meadow.
3.2 Pass by a small spring.
3.9 Arrive at a ridgeline and the Lobo Peak Trail 57; go left.
4.2 Reach a high point on the ridge with spectacular views—the turn-around point.

The trail reaches the first of several long switchbacks at the 1.8-mile mark and begins to pull away from the creek. The next 2 miles are extremely steep as the trail climbs up through a dense, mixed-conifer forest. The trail enters a small meadow surrounded by tall aspen trees at the 3.0-mile mark. This meadow provides brief relief from the steep hiking and is a great spot to take a short break. Past the meadow, the trail begins to climb steeply and passes near a small spring. Just beyond the spring, the trail veers right and climbs steeply straight up the canyon, passing several old pine trees. This section can be a bit confusing, so look for rock cairns and blazes on the trees to help you navigate.

The trail heads to the east and then back west up the final switchbacks before it arrives at a trail junction at the ridgeline and the 3.9-mile mark. Go left on the Lobo Peak Trail, following the edge of the exposed ridge with spectacular views to Wheeler Peak. You'll reach the high point of the ridgeline at mile 4.2, with a rocky perch on the left. After enjoying the impressive and well-deserved views here, you can turn around and retrace your route back to the trailhead.

38 YERBA CANYON

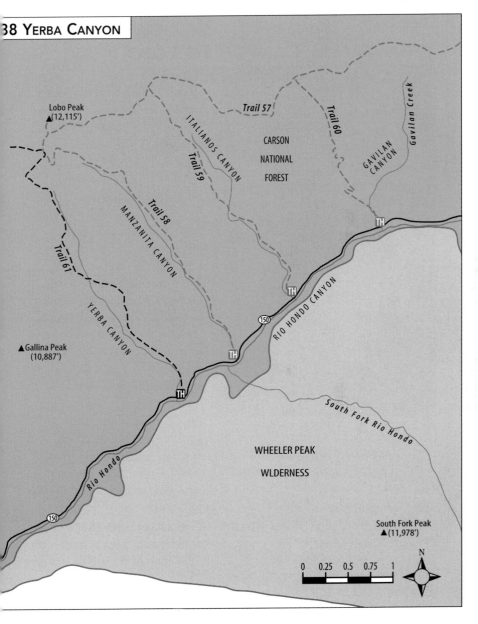

Lobo Peak
▲(12,115')

Trail 57

Trail 60

Gavilan Creek

ITALIANOS CANYON

Trail 59

CARSON

NATIONAL

FOREST

GAVILAN CANYON

Trail 58

MANZANITA CANYON

Trail 61

TH

TH

150

RIO HONDO CANYON

YERBA CANYON

TH

▲Gallina Peak
(10,887')

South Fork Rio Hondo

TH

WHEELER PEAK

WLDERNESS

Rio Hondo

150

South Fork Peak
▲(11,978')

N

0   0.25   0.5   0.75   1

HIKE 39

MANZANITA CANYON TO LOBO PEAK

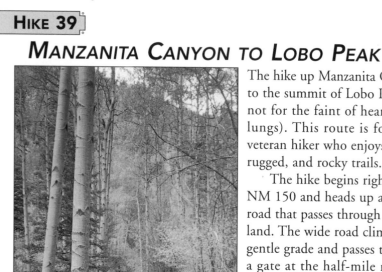

The hike up Manzanita Canyon to the summit of Lobo Peak is not for the faint of heart (or lungs). This route is for the veteran hiker who enjoys steep, rugged, and rocky trails.

The hike begins right off NM 150 and heads up a dirt road that passes through private land. The wide road climbs at a gentle grade and passes through a gate at the half-mile mark. You'll enter a small meadow loaded with wildflowers and willows and proceed to a stream crossing. As the canyon narrows, so does the trail, which parallels the creek, so you'll cross the stream several times before reaching some switchbacks at the 1.5-mile mark.

This is where the fun begins. Climb up the switchbacks along a steep, sloped hill. Strenuous hiking continues through stands of tall aspen trees and mixed conifers. At around the 2.7-mile mark, you'll reach another series of steep switchbacks and a narrow ridge with a stream on the left. The trail climbs along the ridge and reaches another crossing. Go left over the stream, then climb the switchbacks to a junction with the Lobo Peak Trail and panoramic views to the north, south, and east. (Lobo Peak itself is just to the right of the trail.) Go right on the Lobo Peak Trail, and climb along the exposed ridgeline. Be aware of the weather! You do not want to be on this ridge if there is a threat of thunderstorms or lightning. When you reach a junction

MILEAGE/KEY POINTS	
0.0	Trailhead and bathroom.
0.5	Reach a gate.
0.8	The first of several stream crossings.
1.5	The first of several switchbacks.
1.8	Begin a series of long, steep switchbacks.
3.9	Open area with great views.
4.2	Reach a junction with the Lobo Peak Trail 57; go right.
4.7	Arrive on the summit of Lobo Peak.

HIGHLIGHTS:	This steep hike up beautiful Manzanita Canyon should not be missed. Wildflowers are abundant during the summer months, and the views from the summit of Lobo Peak are expansive and spectacular.
DISTANCE:	4.7 miles one way
TRAIL RATING:	Strenuous, with an elevation gain of 3,500 feet
HIKING TIME:	4 to 7 hours
LOCATION:	15 miles northeast of Taos
ELEVATION:	8,400 to 12,115 feet
SEASON:	Late June to late October
MAPS:	Carson National Forest; USGS: Arroyo Seco, Wheeler Peak
MANAGEMENT:	Carson National Forest
DIRECTIONS:	Travel north from Taos on US 64 to NM 150. Turn right on NM 150, and continue 12.1 miles to the trailhead on the left.

with Lobo Peak Trail 57, continue straight for a short distance until you reach the rocky summit.

Lobo Peak is the highest point on the north side of Rio Hondo Canyon and offers spectacular and expansive views in all directions. Enjoy a well-deserved rest, and keep an eye out for thunderstorms. Retrace the route back to the Manzanita Trail and back down the canyon to the trailhead.

39 MANZANITA CANYON TRAIL

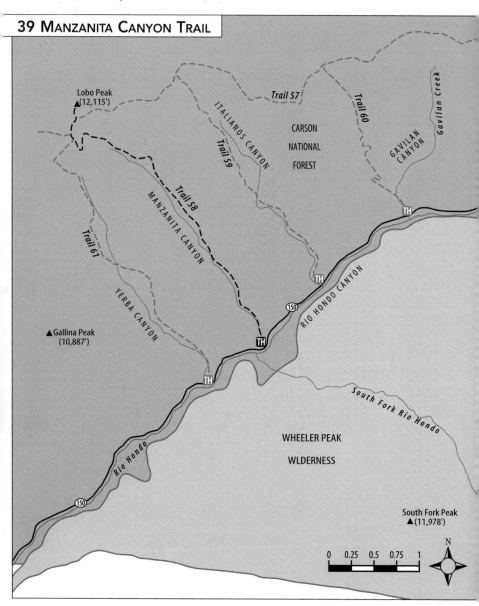

Lobo Peak
▲(12,115')

Trail 57

Trail 60

Gavilan Creek

ITALIANOS CANYON

Trail 59

CARSON

NATIONAL

FOREST

GAVILAN
CANYON

Trail 58

MANZANITA CANYON

TH

Trail 61

RIO HONDO CANYON

TH

150

YERBA CANYON

▲Gallina Peak
(10,887')

TH

TH

South Fork Rio Hondo

Rio Hondo

WHEELER PEAK

WLDERNESS

150

South Fork Peak
▲(11,978')

0   0.25   0.5   0.75   1

N

[handwritten note at top: nice hike, good view of Wheeler from upper meadow, golden aspens, rocks to cross streams, very windy day]

HIKE 40

ITALIANOS CANYON

This is an absolutely beautiful hike into rugged high country just west of the Taos Ski Valley. The trail follows a lovely mountain stream through several aspen meadows that are filled with colorful wildflowers during the summer months. The first mile of the hike makes several stream crossings, with carefully placed logs and rocks to help negotiate the stream. Wildflower lovers will enjoy this section of the hike immensely. Larkspur, bluebell, cow parsnip, and wild rose grow profusely in the moist and fertile soil along the creek.

The trail cuts through a stand of tall and stately aspen at 0.5 mile. Fall colors along this section of the trail are just spectacular. You'll arrive at a stream crossing at the 0.7-mile mark. Use caution crossing the stream, and begin a gentle climb up to another stream crossing, by way of a log bridge, at the 1.2-mile mark. You'll begin a steep climb up to a series of switchbacks at the 1.5-mile mark that leads to another stream crossing. Pass through a mixed-conifer forest before climbing out of the trees and into the first of several beautiful mountain meadows. This is a great spot for a short break. Wildflowers and green meadow grasses grow along with aspen and pine trees here.

Beyond the meadow, the trail climbs steeply back into the forest. (The stream will be on your right.) Another, larger meadow is reached at the 3.0-mile mark, and views open to the south back to Wheeler Peak, the highest point in

MILEAGE/KEY POINTS
0.0 Trailhead.
0.5 Lovely aspen forest.
0.7 Stream crossing.
1.2 Stream crossing via logs.
1.5 Steep switchbacks.
2.4 The first of several lovely meadows.
3.0 Large, open meadow.
3.7 Junction with the Lobo Peak Trail 57 and the turnaround point.

HIGHLIGHTS:	This wonderful trail up into Italianos Canyon passes through several flower-filled meadows and is one of my favorite hikes in the area.
DISTANCE:	3.7 miles one way
TRAIL RATING:	Strenuous, with an elevation gain of 2,800 feet
HIKING TIME:	3.5 to 5.5 hours
LOCATION:	15 miles northeast of Taos
ELEVATION:	8,700 to 11,500 feet
SEASON:	Late June to late October
MAPS:	Carson National Forest; USGS: Arroyo Seco, Wheeler Peak
MANAGEMENT:	Carson National Forest
DIRECTIONS:	Travel north from Taos on US 64 to NM 150. Turn right on NM 150 and continue 12.9 miles to the trailhead and parking on the left.

New Mexico. Travel through the open meadow, and follow the faint trail up through a steep section that gains a small ridge. Veer to the right as you climb through a nice aspen forest to reach Lobo Peak Trail at 3.7 miles. Views open in three directions, and spectacular scenery abounds. Take a well-deserved rest before retracing the route back to the trailhead and your car.

Aspen trees are illuminated by the sunlight.

40 ITALIANOS CANYON

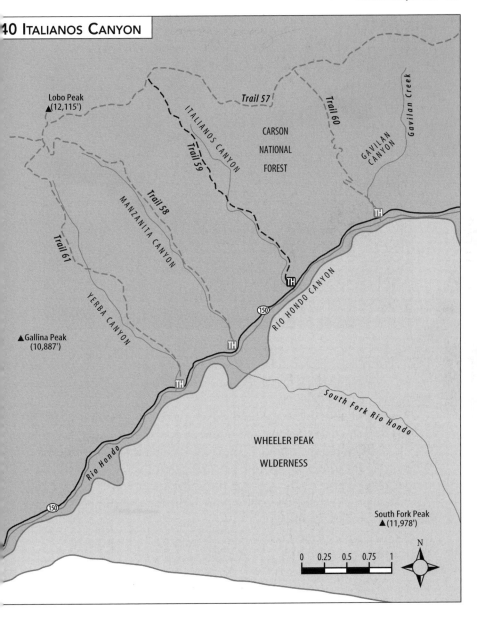

Lobo Peak
▲(12,115')

Trail 57

CARSON

NATIONAL

FOREST

ITALIANOS CANYON

Trail 59

Trail 58

MANZANITA CANYON

Trail 61

YERBA CANYON

Trail 60

GAVILAN CANYON

Gavilan Creek

TH

TH

150

RIO HONDO CANYON

▲Gallina Peak
(10,887')

TH

TH

South Fork Rio Hondo

WHEELER PEAK

WLDERNESS

Rio Hondo

150

South Fork Peak
▲(11,978')

0   0.25   0.5   0.75   1

N

HIKE 41

GAVILAN TRAIL

The Gavilan Trail 60 ascends almost 3,000 feet in less than 3 miles of hiking. The trail parallels lovely Gavilan Creek through meadows, quaking aspen, and stands of conifer.

Enter the woods at the trailhead, passing several private homes on the right. The trail climbs steeply and reaches a gate in just under 0.5 mile. Go left at the gate, and travel along the creek, surrounded by lush vegetation. Wild geranium, wild parsley, cow parsnip, paintbrush, lousewort, and various other plants thrive in the moist soil near the creek. Around the 0.7-mile mark, the trail crosses the stream to the east and climbs up several steep switchbacks. The next mile of hiking is extremely steep and unrelenting as it travels along a hill through mixed conifers.

You'll reach a nice, open meadow filled with lovely aspen—the perfect spot to enjoy a brief respite from the steep hiking. The trail crosses the creek at the top of the meadow. Look up and just to

MILEAGE/KEY POINTS
0.0 Trailhead.
0.4 Reach a gate, go left.
0.7 Stream crossing; begin climbing up steep switchbacks.
1.6 The first of several meadows.
1.9 Small stream crossing. (Look right to find a small spring for a good water source.)
2.1 Climb up a short, steep, rocky gulch.
2.4 Reach a trail junction and the turnaround point.

HIGHLIGHTS:	You just might see a *gavilan*, Spanish for sparrow hawk or kestrel, on this short, steep canyon hike up through wildflower-filled, alpine meadows.
DISTANCE:	2.4 miles one way
TRAIL RATING:	Strenuous, with an elevation gain of 2,900 feet
HIKING TIME:	3 to 5 hours
LOCATION:	15 miles northeast of Taos
ELEVATION:	8,900 to 11,800 feet
SEASON:	Late June to late October
MAPS:	Carson National Forest; USGS: Arroyo Seco, Wheeler Peak
MANAGEMENT:	Carson National Forest
DIRECTIONS:	Travel north from Taos on US 64 to NM 150. Turn right on NM 150 and continue 13.5 miles to the trailhead and parking on the left.

the right of the creek for a small spring shooting out of the hillside. This is a good spot to stock up on cold, refreshing mountain water. Climb up to another meadow, and follow the trail up a steep, rocky slope. You'll soon arrive at another lovely meadow as the trail bears left into the trees. Switchback through the trees to reach a junction with Lobo Peak Trail (Trail 57), Columbine Trail, and the turnaround point for this hike. Take a good rest, and enjoy the gorgeous views south to Wheeler Peak and beyond before retracing the route back to the trailhead.

41 GAVILAN TRAIL

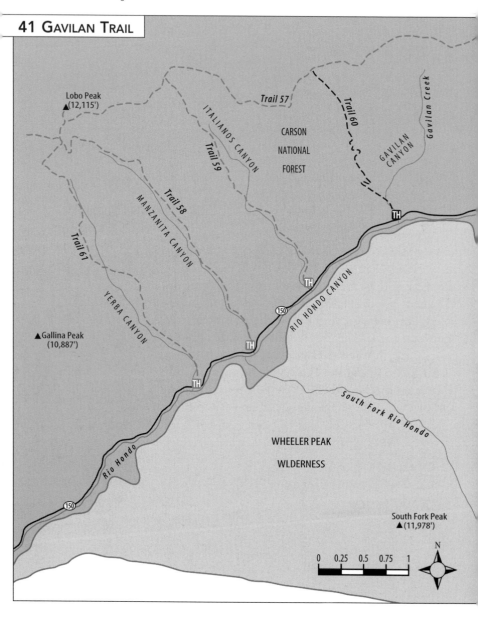

HIKE 42

BULL-OF-THE-WOODS MEADOW

HIGHLIGHTS:	Bring the whole family on this short hike to a wonderful, wildflower-filled meadow.
DISTANCE:	2 miles one way
TRAIL RATING:	Easy to moderate
HIKING TIME:	1 to 3 hours
LOCATION:	15 miles northeast of Taos
ELEVATION:	9,390 to 10,900 feet
SEASON:	Early June to late October
MAPS:	Carson National Forest; USGS: Wheeler Peak
MANAGEMENT:	Carson National Forest/Wheeler Peak Wilderness
DIRECTIONS:	From the intersection of NM 522 and NM 150, travel northeast on NM 150 for 15 miles to the Taos Ski Valley. Turn left into a large parking area near a Forest Service kiosk. The hike starts here.

The hike up to Bull-of-the-Woods Meadow on the Columbine Twining National Recreation Trail 62 is particularly suited for the novice hiker, but outdoor enthusiasts of all abilities will enjoy the beauty

MILEAGE/KEY POINTS

0.0 Trailhead and kiosk.
1.0 Junction with the Long Canyon Trail 63; bear right.
2.0 Reach Bull-of-the-Woods Meadow and turnaround point.

here. The first section of the trail is the most strenuous and can be a bit confusing. The second section follows a wide road with great views out to the Taos Ski Valley and the surrounding hills.

Start the hike by passing the Forest Service kiosk and crossing Twining Road. Follow the trail into the woods, staying on the east side of Rio Hondo's Lake Fork. A bit of strenuous hiking leads you through several open areas to some power lines. The abundant wildflowers that grow along the stream peak during late July and early August.

Around the 1-mile mark, the trail crosses a road and comes to a junction with Long Canyon Trail 63 on the left. Bear right, and you'll soon reach a road going right, back to the ski valley. Follow the main trail straight and begin a nice climb up toward Bull-of-the-Woods Meadow. The road parallels a beautiful meadow on the right, and views open back down to the ski valley and beyond. The hill comes to an abrupt end at a road junction near a pond. (Wheeler Peak Trail goes right and climbs steeply to the summit—the highest point in New Mexico.) Continue straight into Bull-of-the-Woods Meadow. Enjoy some time viewing flowers, looking at the views, or having a picnic before retracing the route back to the trailhead.

42 Bull-of-the-Woods Meadow

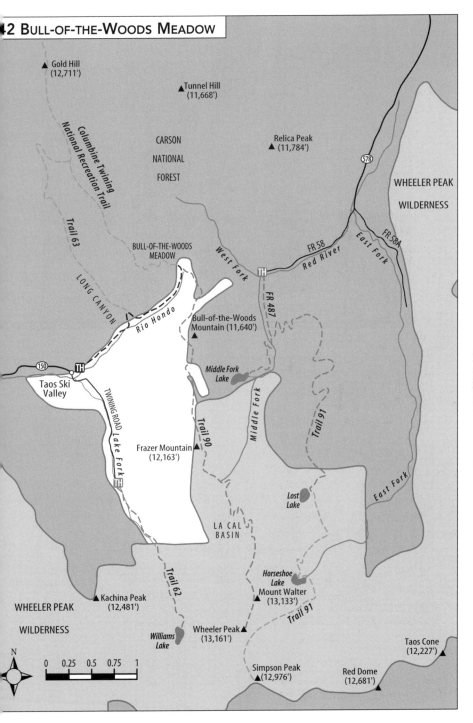

Gold Hill
(12,711')

Tunnel Hill
(11,668')

CARSON

NATIONAL

FOREST

Relica Peak
(11,784')

578

WHEELER PEAK

WILDERNESS

Columbine Twining
National Recreation Trail

Trail 63

FR 58

Red River

East Fork

FR 58A

West Fork

BULL-OF-THE-WOODS
MEADOW

LONG CANYON

Rio Hondo

TH

FR 487

Bull-of-the-Woods
Mountain (11,640')

Middle Fork
Lake

150 TH

Taos Ski
Valley

TWINING ROAD   Lake Fork

Trail 90

Middle Fork

Trail 91

Frazer Mountain
(12,163')

TH

Lost
Lake

LA CAL
BASIN

East Fork

Trail 62

Kachina Peak
(12,481')

WHEELER PEAK

WILDERNESS

Williams
Lake

Wheeler Peak
(13,161')

Horseshoe
Lake
Mount Walter
(13,133')

Trail 91

Taos Cone
(12,227')

N

0   0.25   0.5   0.75   1

Simpson Peak
(12,976')

Red Dome
(12,681')

HIKE 43

WHEELER PEAK

HIGHLIGHTS:	Wheeler Peak is the highest summit in New Mexico. Spectacular views, wildflowers, lovely alpine tundra, beautiful alpine lakes, and the thrill of the rarefied environment will be yours on this long, arduous adventure.
DISTANCE:	7.8 miles one way
TRAIL RATING:	Strenuous
HIKING TIME:	6 to 10 hours
LOCATION:	15 miles northeast of Taos
ELEVATION:	9,390 to 13,161 feet
SEASON:	Early June to late October
MAPS:	USGS: Wheeler Peak
MANAGEMENT:	Carson National Forest/Wheeler Peak Wilderness
DIRECTIONS:	From the intersection of NM 522 and NM 150, travel northeast on NM 150 for 15 miles to the Taos Ski Valley. Turn left into a large parking area near a Forest Service kiosk. The hike starts here.

This is the mother of all mountains in New Mexico and the state's highest peak. There is nothing more exhilarating than standing on an alpine summit surrounded by seemingly endless views. This route should only be attempted by strong hikers who are accustomed to hiking at high elevations and in good physical condition. Although the significant elevation gain is spread out over roughly 8 miles, the last 3 miles are quite steep and travel on an exposed ridgeline that is prone to lightning. Be particularly careful along this section of trail during the monsoon season.

MILEAGE/KEY POINTS

0.0 Trailhead and kiosk.
1.0 Junction with the Long Canyon Trail; go right.
2.0 Arrive at lovely Bull-of-the-Woods Meadow; turn right.
3.0 Reach a gate.
5.0 Arrive at a trail junction in La Cal Basin; go left.
5.2 Cross the stream.
7.6 Summit of Mount Walters
7.8 Summit of Wheeler Peak.

From the parking area, head past the kiosk and cross the road. Trail 90 enters the woods and climbs steeply away from the ski area, staying close to the stream. There is great wildflower viewing along this section of the trail. After a mile of steep hiking, you'll arrive at a junction with the Long Canyon Trail. The Long Canyon Trail goes left and climbs for just under 4 miles to the summit of Gold Hill, but we have bigger fish to fry. . . .

The trail to Wheeler Peak veers right and meets an old logging and mining road on the left. Follow this road up through a beautiful valley and past several flower-filled meadows on the right before arriving at a junction near a small pond. Bull-of-the-Woods Meadow lies straight ahead, but you'll go right and along the road, following the signs for Wheeler Peak. The road begins to climb and veers right near a nice view of Red River on the left.

Continue climbing on the road through a mixed-conifer forest, traversing the west flank of Bull-of-the-Woods Mountain. The road turns into a trail near the 3.1-mile mark, just past a gate. The trail then veers right and travels through a pine forest before breaking into open tundra and heading toward Frazer Mountain. Exposed (watch out for storms) and beautiful hiking will bring you to a ridge just below Frazer Mountain. Wonderful wildflowers line the trail here, adding color to the hearty tundra grass. When you reach a ridge just below Frazer Mountain, you'll have to do the unthinkable—head downhill! It is always demoralizing to loose hard-earned elevation on a challenging hike.

Drop steeply down into La Cal Basin, and you'll arrive at a trail junction near the bottom of the hill. Go left through a bristlecone pine forest (can be snow-covered until August), and cross the Middle Fork of the Red River at its source—a good place to fill your water bottles. By now you have traveled just over 5 miles, and you have almost 2.5 miles of steep hiking left. This is a good spot to rest or to turn around if you are tired or if the weather is of concern.

The trail veers left through a stunted pine forest and then begins a long, *long* climb through the tundra to a ridgeline on the north side of Mount Walter. The beautiful and aptly named Horseshoe Lake lies to your left in a scenic alpine basin. The spectacular hiking along this section makes the effort to get here more than worthwhile.

The summit of Mount Walter is the 7.6-mile mark. Spectacular views spread out in all directions, including a glimpse of picturesque Williams Lake, nestled below and to the west. Continue along the exposed ridge, and you'll arrive at the 13,161-foot summit of Wheeler Peak—mile 7.8 at last! Take photographs, have a snack, and enjoy the wonderful views. Don't linger on the summit if clouds are building, however, as this is *not* the place to be in an electrical storm. When you are rested and ready, retrace your route back to the trailhead.

For an alternate route back to the trailhead, drop back down the ridge toward Mount Walter. Go left down the fall line, dropping a steep and often snow-covered 1.2 miles to Williams Lake. From here, follow the Williams Lake Trail down to its trailhead, then hike back along the road to the Wheeler Peak Trailhead and your car. This is a good bail-out route if storms catch you on the ridge.

Looking down at Horseshoe Lake from Mount Walter.

43 WHEELER PEAK

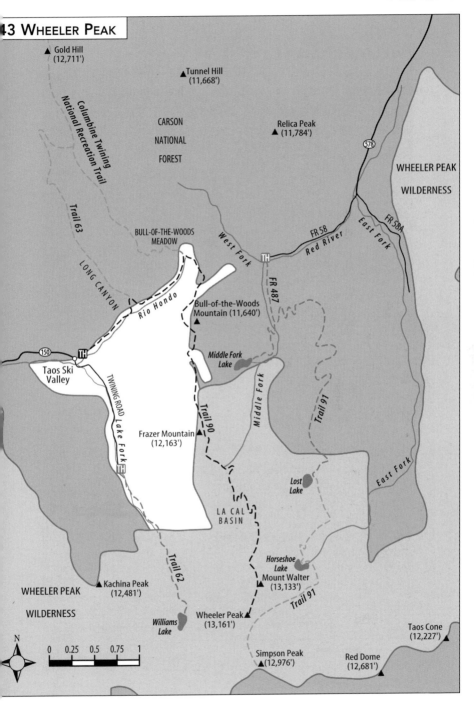

▲ Gold Hill
(12,711')

▲ Tunnel Hill
(11,668')

CARSON

NATIONAL

FOREST

Relica Peak
▲ (11,784')

Columbine Twining
National Recreation Trail

Trail 63

578

WHEELER PEAK

WILDERNESS

FR 58A

BULL-OF-THE-WOODS
MEADOW

West Fork

FR 58

Red River

East Fork

TH

LONG CANYON

Rio Hondo

Bull-of-the-Woods
Mountain (11,640') ▲

FR 487

150

TH

Taos Ski
Valley

TWINING ROAD

Lake Fork

Middle Fork
Lake

Middle Fork

Trail 90

Trail 91

Frazer Mountain
(12,163') ▲

Lost
Lake

East Fork

LA CAL
BASIN

Trail 62

Horseshoe
Lake

WHEELER PEAK

WILDERNESS

▲ Kachina Peak
(12,481')

Mount Walter
(13,133')

Trail 91

Williams
Lake

Wheeler Peak ▲
(13,161')

Taos Cone
(12,227')

N

Simpson Peak
▲(12,976')

Red Dome
(12,681') ▲

0   0.25   0.5   0.75   1

WILLIAMS LAKE

HIGHLIGHTS:	A short, scenic hike leads to Williams Lake, nestled in a rocky, alpine cirque below the towering summit of Wheeler Peak.
DISTANCE:	2 miles one way
TRAIL RATING:	Easy
HIKING TIME:	1 to 3 hours
LOCATION:	15 miles northeast of Taos
ELEVATION:	9,900 to 11,120 feet
SEASON:	Early June to late October
MAPS:	USGS: Wheeler Peak
MANAGEMENT:	Carson National Forest
DIRECTIONS:	From the intersection of NM 522 and NM 150, travel northeast on NM 150 for 15 miles to the Taos Ski Valley. Just before the large parking lot at the base of the ski area, bear left onto Twining Road. Climb up the road (following signs for the Bavarian Restaurant) to reach a parking area on the left with a Forest Service kiosk. The hike starts here.

This is a great little hike for the whole family. The distance is short, the grade is moderate, and kids will love to play along the shore of the lake. Go left from the parking area and kiosk, and head down the road

MILEAGE/KEY POINTS
0.0 Trailhead and parking area.
0.5 Go left at fork.
1.1 Sign marking the Wheeler Peak Wilderness.
2.0 Arrive at beautiful Williams Lake.

toward the Bavarian Restaurant. Pass the restaurant on the left and reach a chairlift. Follow the road along Lake Fork Creek, watching for signs for Williams Lake. You'll go left at the fork. The road soon narrows to a path (Trail 62), and you'll reach a sign indicating that Williams Lake is 2 miles (which is incorrect—it's closer).

The trail now heads into a dense forest of Englemann spruce and then breaks into a little meadow filled with beautiful wildflowers during the summer months. You'll arrive at the sign marking the Wheeler Peak Wilderness at mile 1.1. The trail then veers back into the trees before crossing several avalanche slopes. Downed trees from a recent avalanche covered the trail when I last hiked here, so it might be difficult to follow the trail through this section. When in doubt, stay near the base of the steep slope to the north.

The trail now climbs up through several rocky switchbacks and stays left of a huge boulder field. You'll soon gain a ridge with views of the lake and Wheeler Peak. From here, follow the trail down to the lake and the lovely meadows surrounding it.

Natural Williams Lake is shallow and does not support fish. Camping and campfires are not allowed along the shore to prevent further damage to the fragile area around the lake. This is an extremely popular destination and sees a fair amount of hiking traffic. To enhance your experience, you might want to do this route during the week.

44 WILLIAMS LAKE

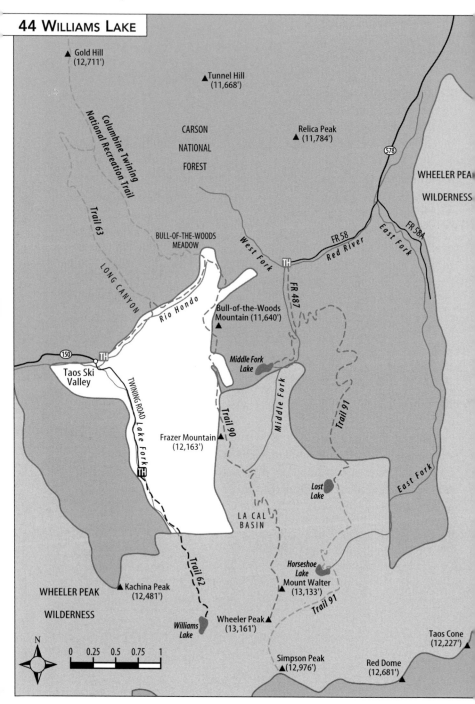

HIKE 45

MIDDLE FORK LAKE

HIGHLIGHTS:	Wildflowers, waterfalls, the rushing Middle Fork of the Red River, and Middle Fork Lake (at 10,845 feet) make this little hike worthwhile, despite the off-road vehicle traffic on the route.
DISTANCE:	2.2 miles one way
TRAIL RATING:	Moderate, with a steady climb up to the lake
HIKING TIME:	2 to 3.5 hours
LOCATION:	6 miles east of Red River
ELEVATION:	9,600 to 11,430 feet
SEASON:	Early June to late October
MAPS:	Carson National Forest; USGS: Wheeler Peak
MANAGEMENT:	Carson National Forest
DIRECTIONS:	Travel south from Red River on NM 578 for 6.2 miles to Forest Road 58. Go right on FR 58 and proceed a rough mile to the trailhead and parking on the right.

I nearly omitted this hike from the book due to the amount of off-road vehicles on the last mile of the route, but the setting and beauty changed my mind. I'd recommend doing this hike early on a weekday morning for the most peaceful experience. Be prepared to encounter ATV and four-wheel-drive traffic as you

MILEAGE/KEY POINTS
0.0 Trailhead and bathrooms. Go right on FR 58.
0.1 Go left on Trail 487/91 over the Middle Fork on a wooden bridge.
0.2 Go right at the first switchback. Follow the Middle Fork upstream on the narrow trail.
1.1 Back on the road; go right.
2.2 Arrive at the lake.

near the lake, particularly if you are hiking on a summer weekend.

Start the hike by going right on FR 58. Reach a gate and small wooden bridge going over the Middle Fork. Go left over the bridge, and begin climbing up the rocky road. When you reach the first switchback, look to your right for a narrow trail leading to the Middle Fork. Take this trail, and begin climbing along the cascading stream. Wildflowers grow wildly along the moist banks of the stream and offer up a kaleidoscope of bright colors during the early summer months.

The trail hugs the stream and clings to the side of the steep hill. At the 1.1-mile mark, the trail climbs up a short hill that dumps you on the road at a junction with the Lost Lake Trail 91 (on the left). Go right on the road and cross the Middle Fork at a small waterfall and wooden bridge. From here, the rest of the hike follows the steep road up to the lake. Be aware of the off-road vehicle traffic as you begin a steep climb up to the lake. The road switchbacks several times and cuts through a dense, mixed-conifer forest.

At the 2.1-mile mark, the road switchbacks again as it climbs a short, steep, rocky hill. When you get to the top, voila! You've reached the lake in its rocky alpine cirque. This is the turnaround point of the hike, so eat some lunch, take some pictures, or, if you brought a fishing rod, spend some time trying to outsmart the cutthroats.

45 MIDDLE FORK LAKE

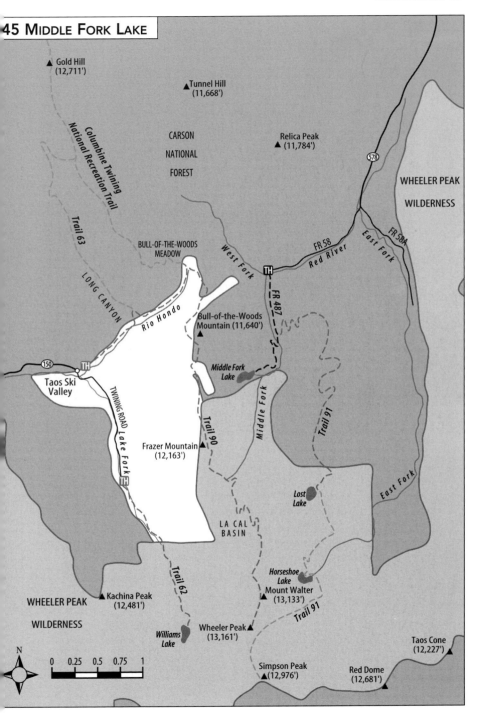

▲ Gold Hill
(12,711')

▲ Tunnel Hill
(11,668')

Columbine Twining
National Recreation Trail

CARSON

NATIONAL

FOREST

Relica Peak
▲ (11,784')

578

WHEELER PEAK

WILDERNESS

Trail 63

LONG CANYON

BULL-OF-THE-WOODS
MEADOW

West Fork

FR 58   Red River

East Fork

FR 58A

TH

FR 487

Rio Hondo

Bull-of-the-Woods
Mountain (11,640')
▲

150

TH

Taos Ski
Valley

Middle Fork
Lake

Middle Fork

Trail 91

TWINING ROAD   Lake Fork

Trail 90

TH

Frazer Mountain
(12,163') ▲

Lost
Lake

East Fork

LA CAL
BASIN

Trail 62

WHEELER PEAK

WILDERNESS

▲ Kachina Peak
(12,481')

Horseshoe
Lake
Mount Walter
(13,133')

Trail 91

Williams
Lake

Wheeler Peak ▲
(13,161')

Taos Cone
(12,227') ▲

N

0   0.25   0.5   0.75   1

Simpson Peak
▲(12,976')

Red Dome
(12,681') ▲

Lost Lake

HIGHLIGHTS:	Another great destination for a day hike or an overnight trip, beautiful Lost Lake is surrounded by high peaks and promises outstanding views.
DISTANCE:	5.0 miles one way
TRAIL RATING:	Strenuous as a day hike, moderate as an overnight trip
HIKING TIME:	4 to 7 hours
LOCATION:	6 miles east of Red River
ELEVATION:	9,600 to 11,430 feet
SEASON:	Late June to late October
MAPS:	Carson National Forest; USGS: Wheeler Peak
MANAGEMENT:	Carson National Forest
DIRECTIONS:	Travel south from Red River on NM 578 for 6.2 miles to Forest Road 58. Go right on FR 58, and proceed a rough mile to the trailhead and parking on the right.

The hike up to Lost Lake is one of my favorites in northern New Mexico. This wonderful excursion on a well-maintained trail ends at a spectacular alpine lake with vast views to the north, east, and south.

Begin by heading right on FR 58 from the trailhead and traveling a short distance to a

MILEAGE/KEY POINTS

0.0 Trailhead and bathrooms. Go right on FR 58.
0.1 Go left over the Middle Fork on a wooden bridge.
1.0 Go left on the Lost Lake Trail 91.
2.5 Reach a ridgeline and views.
4.0 Travel over the first large talus slope.
5.0 Arrive at Lost Lake.

gate. Go left at the gate, and cross over the Middle Fork of the Red River on a sturdy wooden bridge. Follow the rough road up to the first switchback. Bear right onto a narrow trail that hugs a steep hill; the Middle Fork will be on your right. Climb steeply, staying close to the Middle Fork, and reach FR 58 at the 1.0-mile mark, just before the road passes a small waterfall. Go left on the marked Lost Lake Trail 91, and begin a long uphill climb on sweeping switchbacks. The wide, smooth trail cuts through a beautiful mixed-conifer forest. Several spurs exist along this section of the trail and will tempt you to cut some switchbacks. Don't do it! Stay on the main trail and enjoy beautiful hiking through the trees.

At the 2.5-mile mark the trail veers right, cutting through the trees, and reaches an open area with beautiful views to the north and east. It then heads to the right and south. You'll traverse along a steep hill below Frazer Mountain with wonderful views to the south. Travel across two large talus slopes before making a short climb up a steep, rocky slope to the boundary of the Wheeler Peak Wilderness. Drop down through the wind-blown pines, and you'll arrive at beautiful Lost Lake.

The lake, formed by retreating glaciers, is nestled in an alpine cirque below the highest ridge in New Mexico. This area offers some of the most spectacular scenery in the northern part of the state. The lake has a healthy trout population, and it is worth bringing a rod to enjoy a leisurely afternoon of alpine fishing. Day-hikers can enjoy a relaxing lunch before retracing the route back to the trailhead.

There are several good campsites near the lake, but remember that camping is not allowed within 300 feet of the water. Backpackers can easily hike to Horseshoe Lake or climb Wheeler Peak using Lost Lake as a base camp.

46 LOST LAKE

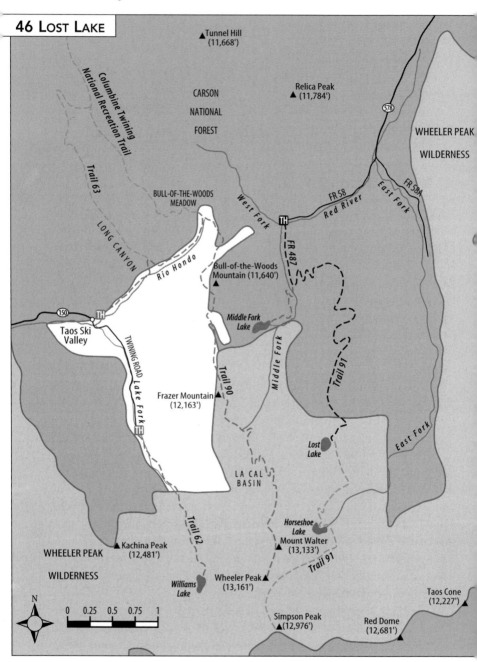

Tunnel Hill
(11,668')

CARSON

NATIONAL

FOREST

Relica Peak
▲ (11,784')

578

WHEELER PEAK

WILDERNESS

Columbine Twining
National Recreation Trail

Trail 63

BULL-OF-THE-WOODS
MEADOW

West Fork

FR 58   Red River

East Fork

FR 58A

TH

FR 482

LONG CANYON

Rio Hondo

Bull-of-the-Woods
Mountain (11,640')

Middle Fork
Lake

150   TH

Taos Ski
Valley

TWINING ROAD   Lake Fork

Middle Fork

Trail 91

Trail 90

TH

Frazer Mountain
(12,163')

Lost
Lake

East Fork

LA CAL
BASIN

Trail 62

Kachina Peak
▲ (12,481')

Horseshoe
Lake
Mount Walter
(13,133')

Trail 91

WHEELER PEAK

WILDERNESS

Williams
Lake

Wheeler Peak ▲
(13,161')

Taos Cone
(12,227') ▲

N

0   0.25   0.5   0.75   1

Simpson Peak
▲(12,976')

Red Dome
(12,681') ▲

HIKE 47

GOOSE LAKE TRAIL

The hike up to Goose Lake and Gold Hill is a wonderful excursion into the high country above the town of Red River. Most of the trails around Red River are open to four-wheel-drive and ATV traffic, but the Goose Lake Trail 65 is essentially a hiking trail with some horse travel during the summer months. Don't let the mileage scare you away from this hike. Whether you choose to hike the first 2 or 3 miles of this trail and enjoy the wildflowers and lovely Goose Creek, or attempt the whole route, you'll appreciate the beauty here.

From the parking lot, cross the bridge and go left along Red River. After a short distance, the trail goes right into a small canyon following Goose Creek. Tall willows and beautiful wildflowers grow profusely during the summer. You'll see a sign for Goose Lake and Gold Hill near a gate and the start of the hike. Pass through the gate and then cross the creek. Reach

MILEAGE/KEY POINTS

- **0.0** Trailhead and bathrooms. Go right on Trail 65.
- **0.5** Pass through a gate.
- **0.6** Cross Goose Creek.
- **2.3** Small open meadow.
- **2.7** Junction with Trail 161 on the right; continue straight.
- **3.3** Reach a trail junction; veer left.
- **3.9** Reach a trail junction; go left.
- **6.0** Arrive at Goose Lake.
- **7.2** Reach the summit of Gold Hill

HIGHLIGHTS:	Beautiful Goose Lake and the alpine summit of 12,689-foot Gold Hill grace this spectacular hike, which can be done as a very long one-day or easier two-day trip.
DISTANCE:	7.2 miles one way
TRAIL RATING:	Strenuous, with a long climb up to Goose Lake and Gold Hill
HIKING TIME:	5 to 10 hours
LOCATION:	2 miles east of Red River
ELEVATION:	8,800 to 12,711 feet
SEASON:	Early June to late October
MAPS:	USGS: Taos County; Carson National Forest
MANAGEMENT:	Carson National Forest
DIRECTIONS:	Travel south from Red River on NM 578 for 2.1 miles to the trailhead and parking on the right at a bridge. The hike starts here.

another gate and cross back over to the north side of the creek. The trail seems to be clinging to the side of the steep hill as it quickly ascends into a mixed-conifer forest. Then it reaches a beautiful aspen-filled meadow at the 2.3-mile mark. This is a nice spot for a short break and flower viewing. The trail slices through the meadow and reaches a junction with Trail 161 on the right, at 2.7 miles. (This trail/road leads back down to Red River.) Continue ahead and into another meadow. I met an outfitter along this section of the trail who was scouting for deer and elk. (I had seen several deer feeding in the meadow but did not relay that information to the guide.)

You'll reach another fork in the trail at the 3.3-mile mark, and veer left into the woods. Beautiful, fairly level hiking through stands of aspen leads into a denser forest of pine. Needles cover the trail and add their sweet fragrance to the fresh mountain air. You'll cross Goose Creek several times as you climb through these pines. When you reach a boggy area, skirt it to the right. The trail climbs up a short, steep hill and then veers right, past a bathroom, and brings you to lovely Goose Lake.

The lake is nestled below Gold Hill and sits 11,000 feet above sea level. Several good sites near the lake make for good base camps if you are going to spend the night and climb Gold Hill the next day. Bighorn sheep roam the rocky slopes surrounding the lakes, and the fishing is quite good for cutthroat trout.

If you're a peak-bagger, follow the trail left (west) along the lake, and follow the ridge as it climbs steeply for a mile to the summit of Gold Hill. Your efforts will be rewarded by beautiful views in all directions. I recommend doing this hike as an overnight trip, so you have plenty of time to enjoy the lake and to climb Gold Hill. Strong hikers can do the whole route in a day; just keep in mind that there is an elevation gain/loss of 4,000 feet!

47 GOOSE LAKE TRAIL

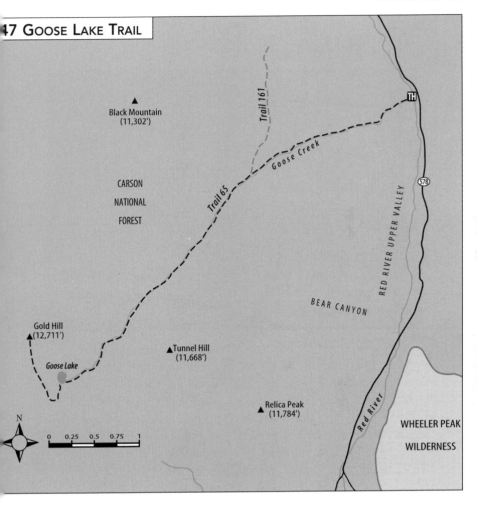

Trail 161

Goose Creek

TH

578

Black Mountain
(11,302')

CARSON

NATIONAL

FOREST

Trail 65

RED RIVER UPPER VALLEY

BEAR CANYON

Gold Hill
(12,711')

Goose Lake

Tunnel Hill
(11,668')

Relica Peak
(11,784')

Red River

WHEELER PEAK

WILDERNESS

N

0   0.25   0.5   0.75   1

HIKE 48

LOBO PEAK TRAIL

This great hike follows San Cristobal Creek for almost 3 miles through a forest of mixed confers and tall, stately aspen. The banks and hillsides along the creek are filled with colorful wildflowers during the summer months, and the fall color here is brilliant gold when the leaves change. The trail cuts up through a narrow canyon and stays in the shade for most of its length. It crosses the creek at least 12 times, so use caution when there is heavy spring runoff. With the exception of some steep spots, this trail climbs at a steady rate and is quite enjoyable.

From the kiosk at the parking area, drop down the wide, double-track trail to a hiker sign at a berm, where the trail meets the creek. Cross the creek and travel up through a forest of mixed conifers, willow, juniper, and mountain mahogany. The trail climbs at a modest rate and crosses the stream several times. Well-placed rocks and logs make the crossings fairly easy and will help keep your feet dry.

At around the 1-mile mark, you'll cross the stream and climb up a short, steep section. During the summer months, keep an eye out for the many

MILEAGE/KEY POINTS
0.0 Trailhead.
0.2 The first of many stream crossings.
1.0 Stream crossing and the start of a short, steep hill.
1.6 Stream crossing and rock wall.
2.0 Arrive at the switchbacks.
3.0 Reach a narrow ridgeline.
3.5 Arrive at a large, open meadow.

HIGHLIGHTS:	This wonderful trail up along San Cristobal Creek leads to a beautiful, flower-filled meadow nestled below Lobo Peak.
DISTANCE:	3.5 miles one way
TRAIL RATING:	Moderate to difficult
HIKING TIME:	3 to 6 hours
LOCATION:	15 miles northeast of Taos
ELEVATION:	8,200 to 10,300 feet
SEASON:	Mid-May to late October
MAPS:	Carson National Forest
MANAGEMENT:	Carson National Forest
DIRECTIONS:	From the junction of NM 522 and US 64, head north on NM 522 for 11.1 miles to County Road 009. Turn right on CR 009 and travel 1.6 miles to San Cristobal. Turn right (just before the post office) and proceed 2.9 miles to a large parking area and the trailhead.

flowers that thrive along the stream. Monkshood, Indian paintbrush, fireweed, rosecrown, gilia, narrowleaf paintbrush, daisies, chiming bells, and cow parsnip can be found growing in the moist soil along the creek. You'll cross the creek at a large rock wall on the left (the 1.6 mile-mark) and begin climbing steeply into a beautiful aspen forest filled with wildflowers. Cross the creek again, on a precarious downed tree, and pass another rock wall on the left.

From here, the trail begins to climb again and soon reaches a series of steep switchbacks. Follow the switchbacks up, pulling away from the stream on a hillside that leads to a narrow ridge. You'll see a small stream babbling along on the left. The trail levels and cuts through a nice pine forest to a beautiful meadow surrounded by aspen and filled with wildflowers during the summer. Several hunting shelters have been built in this meadow, and some nice campsites can be found as well. A small, seasonal stream flows down through the meadows—a good source for water when it's flowing. From here, you can retrace the route back to your car.

The trail continues to Lobo Peak, 2.5 miles beyond the turnaround. The route up to the ridge is difficult to follow, as it cuts through a dense forest with many downed trees. However, on a mid-week hike here, I had the pleasure of complete solitude on this stretch of trail, save for a fair amount of wildlife. Deer, turkey, and ptarmigan were just a few of the animals that crossed my path (or I theirs) on the way to the 12,115-foot summit.

48 LOBO PEAK TRAIL

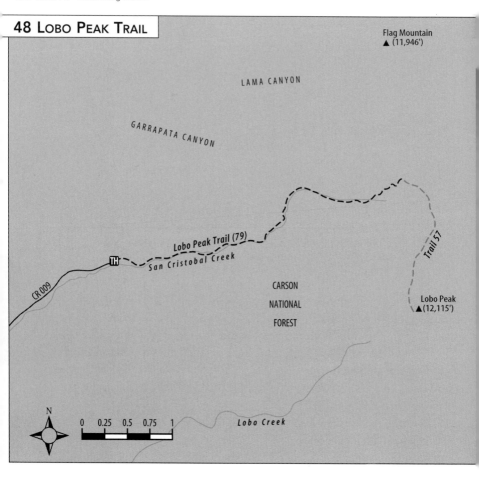

Flag Mountain
▲ (11,946')

LAMA CANYON

GARRAPATA CANYON

Lobo Peak Trail (79)

San Cristobal Creek

TH

CR 009

CARSON

NATIONAL

FOREST

Trail 57

Lobo Peak
▲(12,115')

N

0   0.25   0.5   0.75   1

Lobo Creek

Hike 49

BIG ARSENIC SPRING LOOP

HIGHLIGHTS:	This short, steep hike down into the Rio Grande Gorge boasts excellent fly-fishing, camping, views, and swimming in the river.
DISTANCE:	4.5-mile loop
TRAIL RATING:	Moderate, with a steep climb back to the trailhead
HIKING TIME:	2 to 4 hours
LOCATION:	20 miles north of Taos
ELEVATION:	7,400 to 6,500 feet
SEASON:	Year-round access
MAPS:	USGS: Taos County
MANAGEMENT:	BLM, Taos Resource Office
DIRECTIONS:	From Questa, travel north on NM 522 for 2.6 miles to the marked turnoff for the Rio Grande Wild and Scenic River on NM 378. Take NM 378 to the left for 11.7 miles, passing through the small village of Cerro to the Big Arsenic Spring Campground on the right. The hike starts on the south side of the campground on the canyon rim.

A spectacular hike down into the Rio Grande Gorge and along the wildly flowing Rio Grande. This is beautiful country, with piñon, juniper, and sage on the canyon rim and tall, stately ponderosa pines along the canyon bottom. There are several shelters along the canyon bottom that make for wonderful and remote camping (fee required). This is a nice option for those who like to fish this section of the Rio Grande and enjoy the solitude of this rugged gorge.

MILEAGE/KEY POINTS

0.0 Trailhead, campground, and parking area.

0.6 Go right on a spur trail leading to Big Arsenic Spring.

1.0 Reach Big Arsenic Spring; return to the main trail.

1.4 Continue straight along the river.

2.3 Reach overnight shelters and Little Arsenic Spring.

2.6 Arrive at a trail junction. Go left, climbing steeply out of the gorge.

3.4 Arrive on the canyon rim. Go left on the Riconada Trail.

4.5 Back at Big Arsenic Spring Campground.

Access the Big Arsenic Spring Trail from the campground, and drop steeply into the gorge. The trail loses elevation quickly, and you'll soon arrive at a trail junction at the 0.6-mile mark. Go right, passing several shelters, to reach a large talus slope on the right. Big Arsenic Spring flows out of the talus here and underneath the trail. Turn around, retrace your steps back to the trail junction, and continue straight along the river, surrounded by tall ponderosas and rugged beauty along the canyon floor. Anglers might want to take a break and test their casting skills on the elusive native trout.

The trail passes a shelter and the Little Arsenic Spring at 2.3 miles. This is another nice spot for a quick break. Continue straight to reach a junction with the Little Arsenic Spring Trail at 2.6 miles. Go left up the trail, climbing steeply out of the gorge and gaining over 700 feet of elevation in 0.7 mile.

When you reach the rim of the canyon, go left on the Riconada Trail, which heads north and back to the trailhead at Big Arsenic Campground. This is a perfect fall or spring hike. Hiking the trail during the summer months, however, can be extremely hot and unpleasant. A dip in the cool waters of the Rio Grande might be your saving grace! Do be cautious of the fast-flowing nature of the river.

49 BIG ARSENIC SPRING LOOP

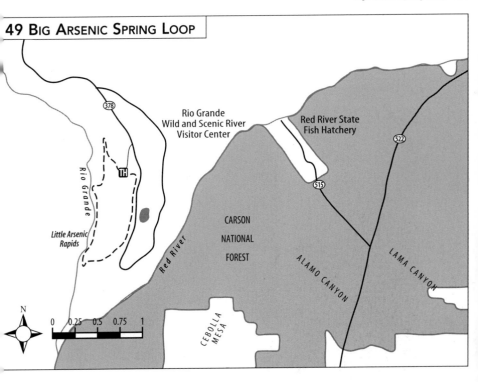

Rio Grande
Wild and Scenic River
Visitor Center

Red River State
Fish Hatchery

378

522

515

Rio Grande

TH

Little Arsenic
Rapids

Red River

CARSON

NATIONAL

FOREST

ALAMO CANYON

LAMA CANYON

CEBOLLA MESA

N

0   0.25   0.5   0.75   1

HIKE 50

GUADALUPE MOUNTAIN

HIGHLIGHTS:	The expansive views from the top of Guadalupe Mountain stretch east to the Latir Peaks, west to the Rio Grande Gorge, and north to the 14,000-foot summits of Little Bear and Blanca Peaks in Colorado.
DISTANCE:	1.8 miles one way
TRAIL RATING:	Moderate, with a steady climb up to the summit
HIKING TIME:	1.5 to 3 hours
LOCATION:	20 miles north of Taos
ELEVATION:	7,400 to 8,232 feet
SEASON:	Year-round access
MAPS:	USGS: Taos County
MANAGEMENT:	BLM, Taos Resource Office
DIRECTIONS:	From Questa, travel north on NM 522 for 2.6 miles, looking for the marked turnoff for the Rio Grande Wild and Scenic River on NM 378. Turn left on NM 378 and proceed 8.3 miles to a dirt road with a sign marking Guadalupe Mountain. Turn left again, and follow the dirt road to a gate, kiosk, parking area, and trailhead. The hike starts here.

The Wild Rivers Recreation Area is one of the best-kept outdoor secrets in northern New Mexico. The free-flowing Rio Grande slices through its deep gorge, flanked by a sage-covered plateau and rounded volcanic hills and peaks. Hiking, fishing, mountain

MILEAGE/KEY POINTS
0.0 Trailhead, small kiosk, and parking.
0.7 Fence line.
0.9 Veer left.
1.1 Great views to the west.
1.2 Arrive at small meadow and a sign; turn right.
1.8 Arrive at the summit of Guadalupe Peak.

biking, and camping are all stellar in this seldom-used area.

Head south from the trailhead. The wide trail climbs a gentle grade and passes through what seems to be an old riverbed. The trail passes a fence line at the 0.7-mile mark and makes an entrance into stands of tall, beautiful ponderosa pines. The road/trail begins to climb steeply, and you'll soon have views to the north and west.

At the 0.9-mile mark the road/trail veers to the left and climbs a steep grade up into a small, beautiful meadow at the 1.2-mile mark. Arrive at a marked trail junction. Take the spur trail to the right for wonderful views of the Latir Peaks, then retrace your route back to the marked junction. Veer left this time, following the narrow trail to a ridgeline. The trail slices through the trees and stays on the ridge until it reaches the summit of Guadalupe Mountain, 8,232 feet above sea level. Expansive views stretch in all directions, and there is a small memorial with candles and other artifacts on the summit.

Enjoy your time at this wonderful spot before retracing the route to the trailhead. On your way back down, you might want to explore the woods to the right of the trail, just before the fence line. Some of the biggest and most beautiful juniper trees I have ever seen are nestled back along the hillside here.

50 GUADALUPE MOUNTAIN

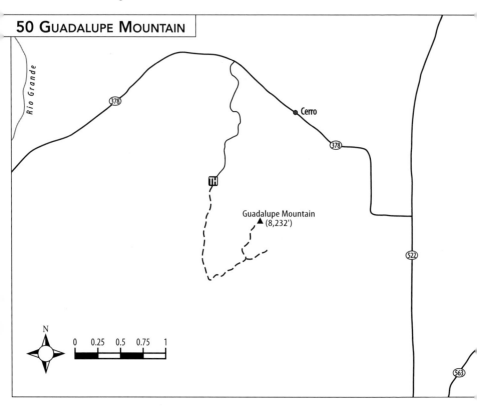

HIKE 51

CEBOLLA MESA TO THE RIO GRANDE

This short hike goes down to the Rio Grande and then follows the river north to its confluence with the Red River. This area is protected as a Wild and Scenic River by Congress, and both rivers flow freely here. The deeply cut gorge, part of the Rio Grande Valley Rift, drops a stunning 800 feet in just one mile of hiking. You will pass through stands of old-growth ponderosa pine—some trees have been here for more than 500 years—and tall, basalt cliffs. Despite the beauty of this area, it sees little foot traffic except for dedicated anglers who make the steep hike in order to enjoy some of the best fly-fishing in northern New Mexico.

Follow the marked trail from the trailhead and campground down into the gorge. Steep switchbacks cut along the hill, dropping you quickly the depth of the gorge. Piñon and juniper trees cling to the steep hill and cacti grow along the sunny west-facing slope. After a half-mile of steep hiking, the trail enters a small, open meadow filled with tall ponderosa pines. This section of trail is exceptionally beautiful, and you might want to take a short break here to enjoy the scenery.

MILEAGE/KEY POINTS

- **0.0** Trailhead, campground, and parking area.
- **0.5** Small meadow and tall ponderosa pines.
- **1.1** The Rio Grande.
- **1.3** Reach the confluence of the Rio Grande and Red River, the turn-around point.

HIGHLIGHTS:	The Rio Grande Gorge offers great fly-fishing, hiking, and swimming, not to mention spectacular views.
DISTANCE:	1.3 miles one way
TRAIL RATING:	Moderate, with a steep climb back to the trailhead
HIKING TIME:	2 to 3 hours
LOCATION:	20 miles north of Taos
ELEVATION:	7,400 to 6,500 feet
SEASON:	Year-round access
MAPS:	USGS: Taos County
MANAGEMENT:	BLM, Taos Resource Office
DIRECTIONS:	Travel north from Taos on US 64 to NM 522. Continue north on NM 522 for 11 miles to Forest Road 9, on the left. Follow FR 9 for 3.3 miles to the trailhead and campground.

The trail then zigzags down to the river and passes by several smooth, black, basalt boulders as it clings to the bank. From here, the route heads upstream to a bridge over the Red River. Stop, sit, and enjoy the fantastic view up the Rio Grande Gorge, accompanied by the sound of the free-flowing river. As I mentioned, the fly-fishing here is quite good, so bring a rod, some lunch, and make a day of it.

This is the turnaround point for the hike, but feel free to extend your mileage by following the trail upriver toward Big Arsenic Spring, a little more than 2 miles away.

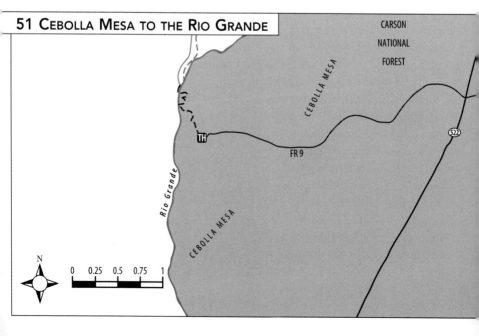

51 CEBOLLA MESA TO THE RIO GRANDE

HIKE 52

HEART LAKE

The Latir Peak Wilderness is a seldom-traveled haven just a few miles from the village of Questa. It is a landscape of mixed-conifer forest, alpine meadows and tundra, lakes and streams, and sweeping ridges linking towering peaks. This is a perfect place for hikers who cherish solitude and beauty.

Start the hike by accessing the Lake Fork Trail 82, just left of the bathrooms. Follow the wide trail along the lake with excellent views to the east. Wildflowers speckle the steep hillsides. Several spur trails (mostly used by anglers) shoot to the right and down to the lake, but stay on the main trail and enter a mixed-conifer forest along Cabresto Creek.

When you reach the boundary of the Latir Peak Wilderness, you'll begin a steady climb through the forest and several small meadows filled with wildflowers during the summer months. At the 2.3-mile mark, you'll arrive at a junction with the Bull Creek Trail 85 and Bull Creek. Veer right across the creek and continue through dense forest on the Lake Fork Trail. The trail veers left at a long switchback and enters into a nice, long meadow with lovely views and great campsites.

At the 3.8-mile mark, the trail cuts through a beautiful pine forest and climbs up to a junction with the Baldy Mountain Trail 81. (The Baldy Mountain Trail goes right and climbs up to Baldy Mountain.) Go left and then angle right on the Lake Fork Trail, climbing

MILEAGE/KEY POINTS	
0.0	Trailhead and bathrooms. Follow Lake Fork Trail 82 along the left (west) of Cabresto Lake.
2.3	Reach a junction with Bull Creek Trail 85. Veer right across creek.
3.5	Open meadow.
4.2	Junction with the Baldy Mountain Trail 81; go left.
4.5	Open meadow and stream crossing.
5.0	Arrive at Heart Lake.

HIGHLIGHTS:	Heart Lake, nestled below towering alpine peaks and mesas, is a lovely destination for a day hike or an overnight trip. Expect beautiful wildflowers during the summer months and great fishing at the lake.
DISTANCE:	5 miles one way
TRAIL RATING:	Strenuous as a day hike, moderate as an overnight trip
HIKING TIME:	3 to 6 hours
LOCATION:	5 miles north of Questa
ELEVATION:	9,200 to 11,473 feet
SEASON:	Late June to late October
MAPS:	Carson National Forest; USGS: Red River, Latir Peak
MANAGEMENT:	Carson National Forest
DIRECTIONS:	From the intersection of NM 522 and NM 38 in Questa, travel east on NM 38 for 0.2 mile and turn left on NM 563. Proceed 2.1 miles and bear right on Forest Road 134. Travel 3.3 miles, turn left on NM 134A, and continue a rough 2.1 miles to the trailhead and the start of the hike at Cabresto Lake.

steeply to an open meadow and Cabresto Creek. The trail becomes faint in the meadow but open to Cabresto Peak, Venado Peak, and the long sweeping ridgeline that connects them.

Climb a short, rocky hill and arrive at a trail junction and beautiful Heart Lake. A small dam on the right takes you to a trail that skirts along the east side of the lake. Excellent campsites exist near the lake for backpackers who want to spend a few days fishing and exploring the surrounding peaks. After you've enjoyed your time at the lake, reveling in the solitude and splendor of this seldom-visited spot, retrace the route back to the trailhead.

52 HEART LAKE

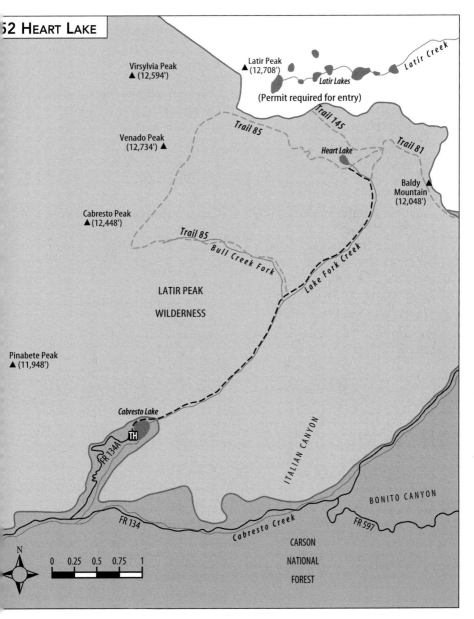

Virsylvia Peak
▲ (12,594')

Latir Peak
▲ (12,708')

Latir Lakes

Latir Creek

(Permit required for entry)

Trail 145

Trail 85

Venado Peak
(12,734') ▲

Heart Lake

Trail 81

Baldy
Mountain
(12,048') ▲

Cabresto Peak
▲ (12,448')

Trail 85

Bull Creek Fork

Lake Fork Creek

LATIR PEAK

WILDERNESS

Pinabete Peak
▲ (11,948')

Cabresto Lake

TH

FR 134A

ITALIAN CANYON

BONITO CANYON

FR 134

Cabresto Creek

FR 597

CARSON

NATIONAL

FOREST

N

0   0.25   0.5   0.75   1

APPENDIX A: CONTACT INFORMATION

SANTA FE

**Santa Fe National Forest
Headquarters**
(1220 St. Francis Dr.)
P.O. Box 1689
Santa Fe, NM 87504
505-988-6940

Espanola Ranger District
P.O. Box 1364
Espanola, NM 87532
505-753-7331

Pecos–Las Vegas Ranger District
P.O. Drawer 429
Pecos, NM 87552
505-757-6121

Bureau of Land Management
P.O. Box 27115
Santa Fe, NM 87502
505-438-7501

**Santa Fe Convention and
Visitors Bureau**
201 W. Marcy St.
Santa Fe, NM 87504
800-777-CITY
www.santafe.org

TAOS

**Carson National Forest
Headquarters**
(208 Cruz Alta Rd.)
P.O. Box 558
Taos, NM 87571
505-758-6200

Camino Real Ranger District
P.O. Box 68
Penasco, NM 87553
505-587-2255

Questa Ranger District
P.O. Box 110
Questa, NM
505-586-0520

Bureau of Land Management
226 Cruz Alta Rd.
Taos, NM 87571
505-758-8851

**Taos County Chamber of
Commerce**
(at the junction of NM68 and
NM585)
P.O. Drawer 1
Taos, NM 87571
800-732-TAOS
www.taosguide.com

APPENDIX B: *BEST OF THE BEST*

BEST WILDFLOWER HIKES

1. Hamilton Mesa
2. Mora Flats
3. Stewart Lake
5. Dockwiller Trail
6. Cave Creek Trail
19. Nambe Lake
20. Puerto Nambe
21. La Vega
22. Santa Fe Baldy
23. Rio en Medio
27. Trampas Lakes
28. Serpent Lake
33. Bernardin Lake
38. Yerba Canyon
39. Manzanita Canyon to Lobo Peak
40. Italianos Canyon
46. Lost Lake
47. Goose Lake Trail
52. Heart Lake

BEST HIKES FOR THE FAMILY

1. Hamilton Mesa
2. Mora Flats
7. Glorieta Ghost Town
12. Dale Ball Trails North
14. Black Canyon Trail
16. Borrego, Bear Wallow,
    Winsor Triangle
24. Tesuque Creek
26. La Vista Verde Trail
33. Bernardin Lake
37. West Rim Trail
42. Bull-of-the-Woods Meadow
51. Cebolla Mesa to the Rio Grande

BEST FALL-COLOR HIKES

1. Hamilton Mesa
2. Mora Flats
17. Aspen Vista
19. Nambe Lake
20. Puerto Nambe
21. La Vega
22. Santa Fe Baldy
27. Trampas Lakes
33. Bernardin Lake
38. Yerba Canyon
39. Manzanita Canyon to Lobo Peak
40. Italianos Canyon
41. Gavilan Trail
43. Wheeler Peak
46. Lost Lake
47. Goose Lake Trail
52. Heart Lake

BEST HIKES FOR ANGLERS

3. Stewart Lake
6. Cave Creek Trail
19. Nambe Lake
27. Trampas Lakes
28. Serpent Lake
45. Middle Fork Lake
46. Lost Lake
49. Big Arsenic Spring Loop
51. Cebolla Mesa to the Rio Grande
52. Heart Lake

Best Hikes for Peak-Baggers

8. Glorieta Baldy Trail
10. Atalaya Mountain
17. Aspen Vista
18. Lake Peak
22. Santa Fe Baldy
35. Devisadaro Peak Loop
43. Wheeler Peak
50. Guadalupe Mountain

Best Hikes for Views

1. Hamilton Mesa
2. Mora Flats
3. Stewart Lake
8. Glorieta Baldy
10. Atalaya Mountain
15. Hyde Park Trail
18. Lake Peak
22. Santa Fe Baldy
26. La Vista Verde Trail
27. Trampas Lakes
28. Serpent Lake
35. Devisadaro Peak Loop
37. West Rim Trail

42. Bull-of-the-Woods Meadow
43. Wheeler Peak
46. Lost Lake
47. Goose Lake Trail
49. Big Arsenic Spring Loop
50. Guadalupe Mountain
51. Cebolla Mesa to the Rio Grande
52. Heart Lake

Best Overnight Hikes

1. Hamilton Mesa
2. Mora Flats
3. Stewart Lake
20. Puerto Nambe
22. Santa Fe Baldy
27. Trampas Lakes
28. Serpent Lake
40. Italianos Canyon Trail
43. Wheeler Peak
46. Lost Lake
47. Goose Lake Trail
49. Big Arsenic Spring Loop
52. Heart Lake

INDEX

Bob D'Antonio is a native of Philadelphia, Pennsylvania, and has spent many hours biking, climbing, and hiking throughout the United States. He has hiked in the mountains of northern New Mexico since 1971, when he first arrived in New Mexico to attend the College of Santa Fe. A well-known rock-climber, Bob has established over 900 climbs in the United States and has authored three rock-climbing guides, several mountain-bike guides, and hiking guides to the Front Range of Colorado and the Indian Peaks Wilderness, near Boulder. Bob loves hiking in the hills of northern New Mexico, often in the company of Laurel, his best friend and wife of 29 years. Today they reside in Louisville, Colorado, along with their three children, Jeremy, Adam, and Rachael, but they hope to return to New Mexico, for the people, the land, the light, and the beautiful simplicity of living in this enchanting land.